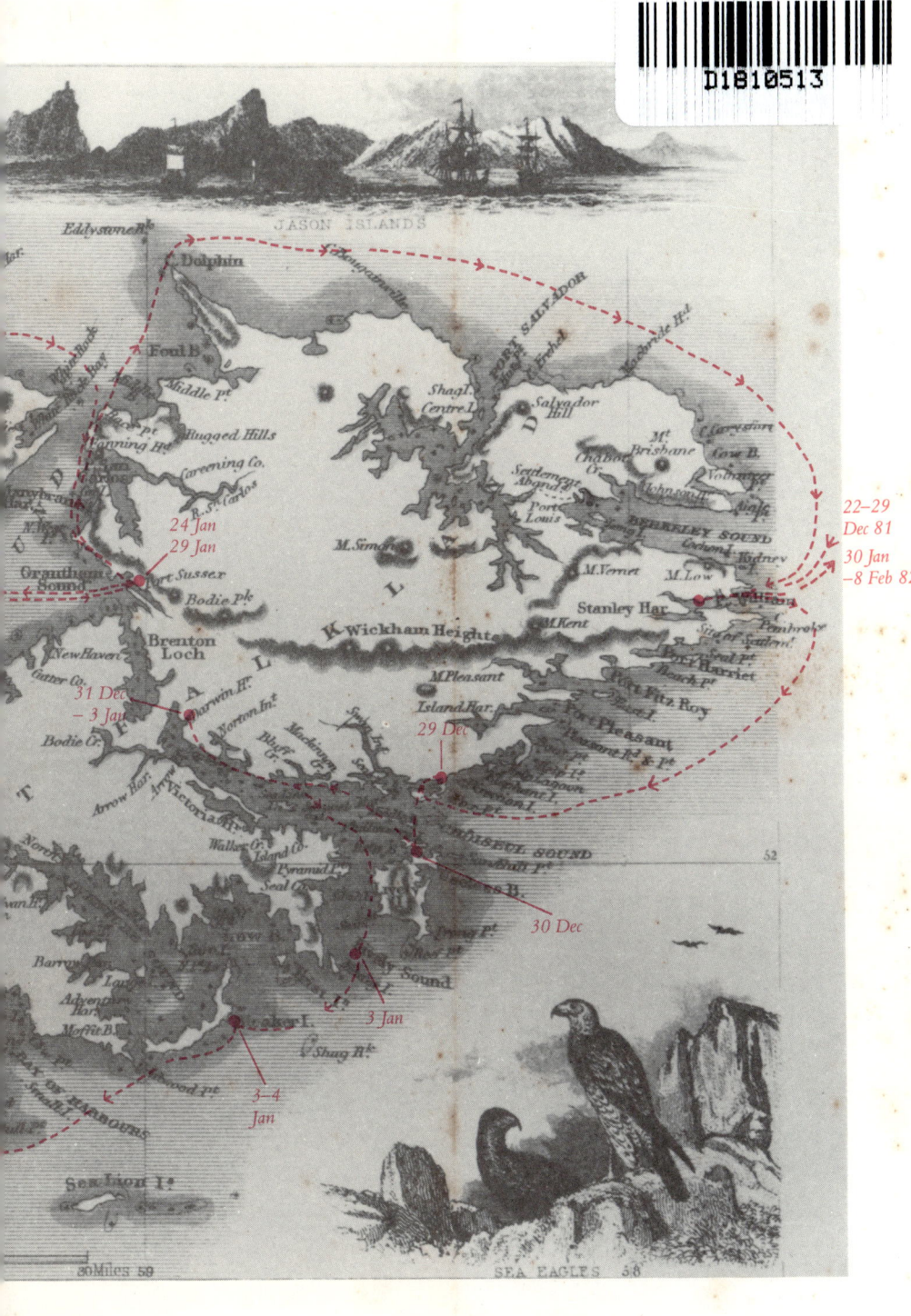

D1810513

JASON ISLANDS

Eddystone R^k

Dolphin

Foul B^a

Middle P^t

Rugged Hills

Careening Co.

Fanning P^t

R. St Carlos

Shag I.
Centre I.

Salvador
Hill

FORT SALVADOR

Mt
Brisbane

Chabod
Cr.

Seedment
Abard^n

Port^o
Louis

BERKELEY SOUND

Carysfort

Cow B.

Johnson^o

Vobringe^o

24 Jan
29 Jan

M. Simon

Grantham
Sound

Port Sussex

Bodie P^k

M. Vernet

M. Low

Kidney

Ceder I.

Stanley Har

Pembroke^o

Brenton
Loch

New Haven^o

Cutter Co.

K. Wickham Heights

Mt Kent

Sugar I.
Harbour

Port Harriet
Beach p^t

Port Fitz Roy

31 Dec
— 3 Jan

Darwin H^r.

Norton In^t

M. Pleasant

Island Har.

Port Pleasant

Bodie Cr.

Arrow Har.

Victoria H^r.

Bluff
Cr.

Mackeury
Cr.

29 Dec

Walker Cr.

Island Co.

Pyramid P^t

Seal Cr.

CHOISEUL SOUND

Marshall P^t

52

30 Dec

North^n

Barrow

Long

Adventure
Hav^n

Moffit B^y

Sound

Prince P^t

3 Jan

3 Jan

Shag R^k

3–4
Jan

Sea Lion I^s

30 Miles 59

SEA EAGLES 58

22–29
Dec 81

30 Jan
—8 Feb 82

The Falklands and The Dwarf

The Cruise of H.M.S. Dwarf
in the Falkland Islands 1881–1882

Also by Kit Layman
Man of Letters (1990)

THE FALKLANDS AND THE DWARF

THE CRUISE OF H.M.S. DWARF
IN THE FALKLAND ISLANDS 1881–1882

by
Rear Admiral C. H. Layman, CB, DSO, LVO
and
Jane Cameron, BA(Hons)

THE FALKLANDS AND THE DWARF

© *Kit Layman and Jane Cameron*
First published in 1995
Picton Publishing (Chippenham) Limited
ISBN 0 0948251 76 X

Designed and typeset in Bembo from Author's discs by
Mike Kelly Phototypesetting,
Biddestone, Chippenham, Wiltshire SN14 7EA
Printed and bound in the United Kingdom by
Picton Publishing (Chippenham) Limited
Queensbridge Cottages, Patterdown,
Chippenham, Wiltshire SN15 2NS
Telephone: (0249) 443430

All rights reserved
No part of this book may be reproduced,
stored in a retrieval system or transmitted, in any form
or by any means, electronic, mechanical, photocopying,
recording or otherwise without the express written
permission of the copyright owners.

PICTON PUBLISHING (CHIPPENHAM) LIMITED

Commander Sir William Wiseman, Bart., Royal Navy
Commanding Officer, H.M.S. *Dwarf* 1881–1882

(Photo: Wiseman Collection)

v

For Janet Martin
granddaughter of Sir William Wiseman of the Dwarf

CONTENTS

LIST OF ILLUSTRATIONS

Acknowledgements

Without the generous access to the Wiseman papers given by Mme Raoul Martin and Sir John and Lady Wiseman this book could not have been written. We are profoundly grateful to them.

For general help and encouragement we are indebted to Mrs Joy Donner, Mr John Smith, and Mrs Joan Spruce.

For information and permission to use photographs and other material we would like to thank Mr Patrick Armstrong, Mrs Kitty Bertrand, Miss Madge Biggs, Mrs Sally Blake, Mr and Mrs Tony Chater, The Falkland Islands Company, The Falkland Islands Museum, Commander Tony Goodhart, Mrs Eileen Jaffray, Mr John Leonard, Dr Jim McAdam, The Merlin Press, Mrs Betty Miller, Mr Roddy Napier, Mr Robin Pitaluga, Mr and Mrs Peter Robertson, Mr Alastair Service of Seeley Service and Co Ltd, and Miss Betty Stronach.

Miss Kathleen Stewart and Miss Sam Ford have put our manuscript together with great professional skill. Mr Frank Walton generously assisted with photographic services and advice. Mr Graham Henderson kindly provided technical support. Miss Janice Brebber took control of the word-processor when discipline seemed to breaking down.

FOREWORD

by

The Rt Hon Douglas Hurd, CBE, MP
Secretary of State for Foreign and Commonwealth Affairs

In 1881 William Wiseman was at the age of 36 given the command of HMS *Dwarf*, with four guns and a crew of 85. He was despatched to the Falkland Islands to enforce a new ordinance establishing a closed season for sealing. Admiral Layman and Jane Cameron have here edited the loving letters which he sent home to his wife in England, filling in the background from their own knowledge.

Jane Cameron told me of the project when I was in the Falklands in April 1994. I did not know quite what to expect – a labour of love certainly, but maybe something quaint, for the specialist. Instead we have a lively and fascinating portrait of the Islands and many of the fifteen hundred Islanders. Commander Wiseman found them at a turning point, and his own experiences covered both past and future. The Victorian age with its contrasts had reached the Islands – dull dinners at Government House, the rumbustious Darwin races, the Bishop sending the sailors to sleep with his sermon, the hymns from Ancient and Modern carefully listed in the letters home, the farmer's wife in her Sunday best exclaiming over the guns on HMS *Dwarf*, the growing professionalism of the wool trade. But not far in the background is a more savage society – the wild bulls which have to be shot as rivals to the sheep, the wrecks in Port Stanley harbour, the family who knew it would take eighteen months to receive a reply to a letter sent to Scotland, the sinister Yankee sealer protesting that he had not murdered one of his crew, the tale of the eight Portuguese who froze to death on South Georgia waiting for the next sealing season.

Commander Wiseman wrote with a vivid straightforward style which is attractive and convincing. His letters, admirably edited, are a real find, and not just for the descriptions of the past. For most of the letters deal with those characteristics of Falkland life which are splendidly unchanged – the unfrightened sealions and seals, the penguins, the amazing variety of all birds, the tussac grass, the rocky shores and the wind.

DOUGLAS HURD

INTRODUCTION

"I think we shall have a very interesting trip to the Falklands," said Commander Sir William Wiseman in a letter to his wife, "as we go to the West Island where hardly anyone has been except sealers and such-like ruffians."

Throughout the history of these extraordinary islands this has often been the view of the first-time visitor, intrigued by the Falklands' reputation for isolation, wild life, wild people, and extreme remoteness. But the visitor usually finds the reality interestingly different from the expectation, and this is what we can see unfolding as we read these letters.

They were written at an important moment in Falkland Islands history, one which has not been well documented. "The year 1881 was a prosperous one for the Colony," noted Governor Thomas Kerr with satisfaction, in his annual report to the Colonial Office. He had every reason to be pleased. In barely forty years he and his predecessors had contrived to transform a fragile settlement of some fifty souls, eking out a precarious living reliant on wild cattle and passing ships, into a stable community of fifteen hundred people enjoying the economic benefits of a rapidly expanding sheep-farming industry and the newly-gained assurance of regular contact with the outside world.

The British government had appointed the first civilian governor to the Islands in 1841, with the idea of developing a settlement which would be useful to British shipping as a port of refuge, repair, and re-provisioning, in a part of the world notorious for the destructive storms which blew around its remote and largely unpopulated shores. Lt. Governor Richard Moody had to contend with a chronic shortage of funds in his early endeavours, and an unpromising collection of colonists, "many men of reckless character, irregular passions, unchecked by any moral impulses, still less discipline," as he reported to London. There seemed to be little hope of economic self-sufficiency for the Islands, whose total income, gained from the sale of beef to passing ships and the export of "hides, seal skins, and a few barrels of oil" barely exceeded a thousand pounds.

Over the succeeding years, however, as life became better organised, three main sources of revenue emerged which between them were to establish the colony on a more solid footing. The first of these was wool. Governors had seen the potential of sheep-farming from the beginning. "There can be little doubt," wrote Moody, "that sheep-farming would answer well... as there is an abundance of nutritious pasture." New settlers were encouraged to pursue this course, and thanks to the hardiness and perseverance of the pioneering farmers, who established flocks and settlements under the most remote and rigorous conditions, by the time of Wiseman's visit wool had eclipsed all other sources of income in value, and sheep-farming had become firmly established as the principal industry.

Production leapt, helped by good wool prices, from £35,000 worth in 1878, to £55,000 worth in 1879, to £68,000 worth in 1880, almost ten times the revenue produced by hides, the nearest rival. So the sheep-farmers that Wiseman encountered on his travels, among them Cobb, Felton, Packe, Holmested and Dean, would understandably have been in a buoyant and hospitable frame of mind.

For the population of Stanley, however, it was ship repair and salvage which provided a living for most people during the middle years of the century. An indication of the value of this work may be gained by a comparison of wages. The Blue Book for 1881 shows that where shepherds and sailors earned £50 a year, shipwrights, blacksmiths, joiners and sailmakers charged anything up to £1 per day, and could therefore earn far more when business was brisk.

A comparison made in 1873 with wages for men similarly occupied in England showed that skilled craftsmen in Stanley earned up to six shillings a day more than their English counterparts, a considerable sum at that time, and a clear indication of a captive market, where ships in distress after a rough passage round Cape Horn had no option but to put into the Falkland Islands. Governor Kerr remarked on the inflated wages in his report for 1880, adding that "the masters of ships however complain more of the idleness of the men, who never do a fair day's work, than of the rate of wages."

Twenty-two vessels in distress arrived for repair in 1881, and Governor Kerr reported that "much profit was derived from the repairs of so many disabled ships in Stanley harbour, on which the artizans of Stanley found full employment at high wages throughout the year." However this year appears to have been unusually busy. In 1876 Governor D'Arcy had already reported a falling off in the number of distressed vessels arriving. He commented that "the stringent orders of the Board of Trade have prevented old vessels from attempting the passage round Cape Horn." He also reported "the number of vessels rounding the Horn has considerably decreased since the wheat trade from San Francisco to Europe, which promised at one time to employ so many British vessels, is now conveyed by the railway over the continent of North America." The following year Governor Callaghan commented: "It is believed many more ships which sustain damage on their homeward voyage round Cape Horn would call here for repairs only that there is no dock at Stanley, a fact which is generally known to the mercantile marine. Under these circumstances the captains prefer struggling on to Montevideo, where all the necessary facilities for repairs can be obtained."

The ship-repair trade never did recover, and by the turn of the century, steamships, so much less vulnerable to the elements, were taking the place of sailing ships. The opening of the Panama Canal in 1914 dealt a final blow to the aspirations of Stanley as a centre for shipping.

It was the sealing trade that brought Wiseman, and H.M.S. *Dwarf*, to the Falklands. Since the earliest years of the colony, seal skins and seal oil, together with penguin oil, had been staple items of export. But in 1872 Governor D'Arcy reported "the collapse of the sealing trade, the supply of those animals having been exhausted in these seas." Five years later Governor Callaghan remarked that "it is greatly to be regretted that a close season was not rendered compulsory." In 1879 however, he noted "a very decided revival of this industry, which for some years past had almost been abandoned by the inhabitants of these Islands."

These events were considered by Governor Kerr who had recently heard reports of the arrival of several American sealers in West Falkland. The necessity for a close season to conserve a valuable resource was obvious and urgent, and he determined to enact a bill restricting sealing to certain months. But without a warship to patrol the Islands and

3

enforce the restrictions sealing captains would neither know nor care about conservation measures passed by the Falkland Islands Legislative Council. The Governor therefore wrote to the Senior Officer of the South East American Station, Captain Loftus Jones, who was based at Montevideo, requesting a visit from the navy. Captain Jones replied that H.M.S. *Dwarf* was on her way.

By 1885 Governor Kerr was reporting that "visits of Her Majesty's ships during the close season of the fisheries has benefitted the Colony, not only by the protection which is given against any attempt to infringe the law, but by the considerable sums of money which are spent in Stanley during these visits. The crews of the ships invariably behave well and are on very friendly terms with the townspeople."

The general aspect of the population appeared to have improved out of all recognition since Moody wrote of the "reckless characters" abounding in 1842. Governor D'Arcy concluded his report in 1876 "by testifying that the inhabitants of the Falkland Islands are energetic and industrious in their personal undertakings; they do not confine themselves to one branch of industry, circumstances have compelled them to change their means of gaining a livelihood, and they suit their occupation to the exigencies of the moment in a manner most profitable to themselves; the conduct of the inhabitants, their amenability to the laws, is most praiseworthy, any violation of the peace being usually of a very unimportant nature, and exceedingly rare."

Although life was undoubtedly easier and more comfortable in the 1880s than it had been in earlier days, it was still rigorous, and called for hardiness and adaptability, particularly from those living in isolated "camp"[1] houses. Of the 1,339 people who according to the 1881 census were British by birth, a large proportion would have been of Scots origin, encouraged to settle here because of their experience of hill-farming and crofting. Of the 158 foreigners listed, the majority came from North European countries, principally Norway, Sweden and Germany. Many of them would have been sailors, who had either become stranded here, or stayed from choice after shipwreck or illness. Charles Hansen, the "very nice fellow" encountered by Wiseman on Carcass Island, was one such.

---

[1] *Camp* is the term used to describe all land in the Falklands outside Stanley. It comes from the Spanish word *campo*, meaning countryside.

As far as the amenities of civilised life went, there were three churches and three schools in the colony (all on East Falkland), but when it came to hospitals, newspapers or banks, the Annual Reports continued to record "There is none" in tones of melancholy emphasis.

Then, as now, the lack of the facilities that the rest of the world took for granted was balanced by the isolated beauty of the landscape and the abundant wildlife that Wiseman so much enjoyed.

★   ★   ★

Sir William Wiseman came from an interesting line. In his family church of Great Canfield, Essex, is a tomb with the effigies of a man and six boys with a woman and six girls. It bears the inscription "Here lyeth John Wyseman, esquier, sometyme one of the auditors of our Soveraigne lord Kynge Henry th' eight of the revenues of the Crown, and Agnes his Wife, which John dyed Aug 17 1558." His descendant, William Wiseman, was created a baronet in 1628 by Charles I and was High Sheriff of Essex. In the same church another descendant lies holding the hand of his lady, while the inscription informs us that she "put off the troublesome robe of mortality the 11th day of May 1662, leaving the four and twentieth year of her age unfinished, whose body lies here mortgaged to the grave until the grand jubilee, the resurrection."

Throughout the nineteenth century the family were active in the naval service. Wiseman's father came to the Falklands in 1834 as a midshipman in H.M.S. *Sparrowhawk*. His ship anchored in Port Louis, where the main settlement had recently been established; it was not until ten years later that the settlement moved to its present location at Port Stanley. He wrote home to his mother "We had beef steaks at Port Louis, a change from living off salt junk for a month. We have laid in a large stock of beef for the voyage" – which was to take them on to Chile and Peru.

But not everything went well during *Sparrowhawk's* visit, which seems to have been plagued by misfortunes with boats. Midshipman Wiseman wrote in his journal "The cutter was upset in a heavy snow squall with all the midshipmen in her, resulting in her going on shore." Another ship's boat was ordered to circumnavigate East Falkland, which in mid-winter would certainly have been a challenge. In the event the boat was wrecked in the vicinity of Eagle Passage at the southern end of

Lafonia, and a crew member, James Robertson, drowned. The remainder had to struggle back overland, a distance of 120 miles. "Mr Hayes Midshipman was brought on board quite exhausted," Wiseman confided to his journal, "having eaten nothing but shellfish and part of Lieutenant Harman's dog since the loss of the boat a month ago."

★   ★   ★

William Wiseman of the *Dwarf* was born in 1845, went to school in Switzerland, and at the age of fourteen followed his father into the navy as a midshipman in H.M.S. *Bacchante*. Four years later he was on the Australian Station, serving under his father who was now a commodore and the Commander-in-Chief. The Maori War broke out in 1863, and both father and son distinguished themselves at their own levels. The Commodore gained much credit and a knighthood for his resolute support of the army which had been pinned down by resourceful and courageous opponents. He formed a Naval Brigade, and transported them up the rivers in a shallow-draught paddle-steamer, H.M.S. *Pioneer*, to relieve the hard-pressed soldiers. The young Wiseman was part of this brigade, fought bravely, and was slightly wounded. He was promoted to Lieutenant, and awarded the New Zealand medal.

Three years later Lieutenant Wiseman was commanding his father's old flagship, the *Pioneer*, on the west coast of Africa. He was ordered to proceed up the river Niger as far as practicable in support of British trading posts, and observe and report the conditions he found ashore. The mission was a purely peaceful one and seemed straightforward, but it nearly ended in disaster. Because of sandbanks and other obstacles progress was very slow, and the ship's company started to go down with "fever and ague" – the dread of every west-coast captain. Six hundred miles up river the *Pioneer* could go no further and she turned back, but the water level had dropped and the return journey was even slower. When she finally reached Ascension Island all but four of the men were sick, and Lieutenant Wiseman himself was subsequently invalided home to recuperate.

In 1871 he was promoted to commander, and soon after inherited the baronetcy when his father, by now a Rear Admiral, died in obscure circumstances in America. His next command was H.M.S. *Lapwing* on the China Station. In her he had a busy four years' commission, observing an eclipse of the sun while staying with the King of Siam, pursuing

Midshipman William Wiseman, Royal Navy

Wiseman joined the navy at the age of fourteen. This photograph was taken just before the Maori War of 1863, when he became part of the Naval Brigade which was formed by his father, the Commander-in-Chief, and transported up river in a shallow-draught paddle-steamer. He fought bravely, and was slightly wounded.

Photo: Wiseman Collection

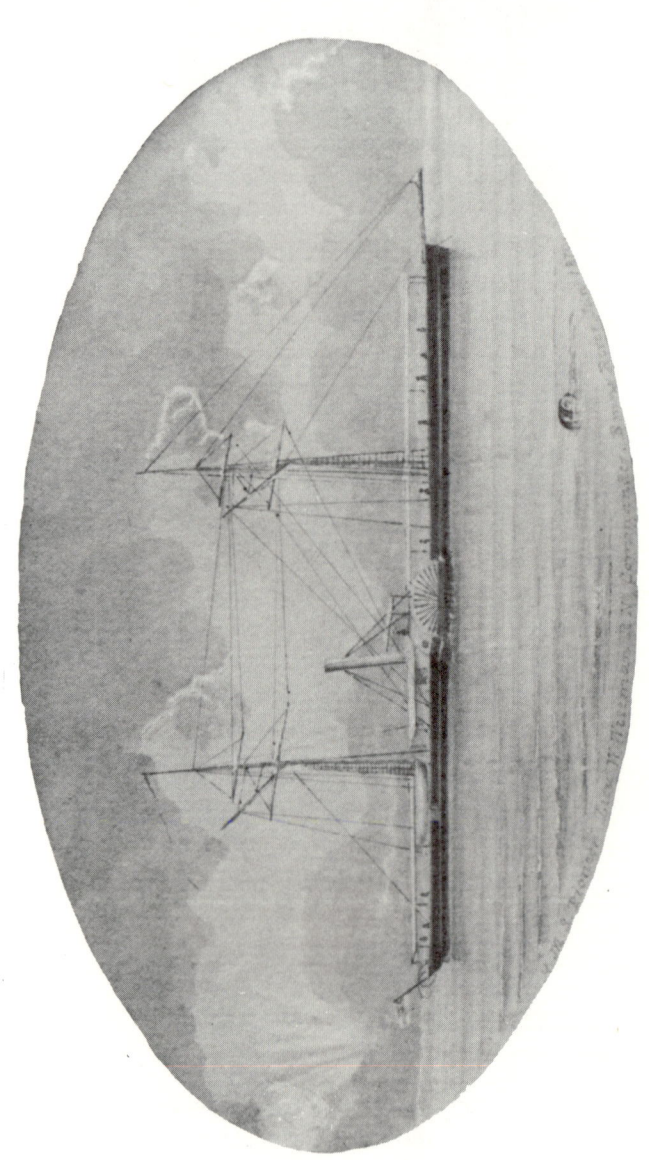

"The *Pioneer*...nearly ended in disaster" (page 6)

H.M.S. *Pioneer*, a shallow-draught paddle-steamer, was flagship to the Commander-in-Chief Australian Station (Commodore Sir William Wiseman) and played a key role in the Maori War of 1863. Three years later she was commanded by Sir William's son, Lieutenant William Wiseman, and nearly became a permanent part of the landscape of the Upper Niger.

Painting by unknown artist from the Wiseman Collection.

8

"Caught by a typhoon and driven fast ashore..." (page 11)

H.M.S. *Lapwing* (Commander Sir William Wiseman) is in serious trouble on the China coast, as this drawing by her First Lieutenant shows. But after a classic salvage operation the ship was refloated 24 days later, and her captain subsequently commended by the Admiralty.

Drawing by H.N. Shore

9

H.M.S. *Dwarf* in Stanley Harbour 1882

Photo: Wiseman Collection

This is the photograph taken by Mr Cobb and referred to on page 147. *Dwarf*, of 600 tons with sails and twin screws, was classed as a Composite Gun Vessel of 4 guns. Her complement was ten officers and warrant officers, and 75 ship's company. In addition there was a ship's dog, and, according to her captain, a goat that was exceedingly fond of rum.

pirates, surveying the rivers of Malaya, and investigating the disposition – friendly or otherwise – of the native princes and chiefs. En route to Tientsin he was caught by a typhoon and driven fast ashore on Changshan Island. His First Lieutenant's drawing of this incident[2] indicates the seriousness of the situation. But good seamen are resourceful, particularly when there is really no alternative. They laid out all available anchors and cables, and landed on the beach everything movable, including masts, coal, condensers, engines, and the six-and-a-half ton gun. Meanwhile five hundred coolies were hired to fill sacks with sand and build around the ship a huge cofferdam, which both protected her from the pounding of the waves, and also enabled them to dig out the shingle from under her. After 24 days aground she was refloated, damaged but repairable. Captains seldom gain credit for going aground, but on this occasion Wiseman was commended by the Admiralty for an exceptional salvage operation.

In 1881 he was appointed to command H.M.S. *Dwarf*, a name which must be among the more curious in the annals of the Royal Navy, inviting attention, it seems, to her small size (160 feet length overall) and somewhat ungainly lines.[3] *Dwarf* was classed as a Composite Gun Vessel, *composite* signifying that she was powered by twin screws as well as sails, and *gun* referring to her four guns, a 100–pounder, a 64 and two 20s. Her total complement was 85 officers and men, and she had been commissioned at Portsmouth two years previously for service on the South East America Station.

Wiseman took passage from England in a British passenger ship, S.S. *Derwent*, bound for Montevideo where he went on board his new command. It is here that we join him, seeing for the first time his ship, his officers, his living quarters. *Dwarf* is to sail for the Falklands almost at once, and Commander Wiseman must quickly discover the sailing and steaming characteristics of his ship, get to know his ship's company, carry out gun drills, and read all the new regulations, reports, and returns. He is an experienced officer, and his letters radiate confidence and competence. But his immediate concern is that the mails are all

---

[2] See page 9.
[3] But still a name of some distinction. The first HMS *Dwarf* was in 1843 the first screw vessel to be commissioned into the Royal Navy. A subsequent *Dwarf* had a busy time in the First World War.

11

going wrong. Like many a naval husband before and since, he is anxious about his wife being anxious.

He seems to have been a cheerful and agreeable ship-mate, and as with most captains of ships in all ages, somewhat autocratic. One of the *Dwarf* officers wrote in his journal "our captain only joined us two days ago. Sir William Wiseman is a little man, and very pleasant at present, but strict." He was fond of amateur dramatics, fond of good company, and passionately fond of shooting.

These genial, perceptive, and loving letters to his wife, often written late at night and always straight from the heart, give us a unique glimpse of both the Falkland Islands and the Royal Navy of that unsung age.

CHAPTER 1

DEPARTURE FROM MONTEVIDEO

H.M.S.*Dwarf*
Monte Video
December 3rd 1881

Dearest wife,

I arrived yesterday at noon and found here *Dwarf*, *Garnet*, and *Firefly*. I came on board here to find that I am to be sent off to the Falkland Islands in three or four days, so I fear I shall miss the mail. What a blow! It is very hard. I will find out what dates I can write to you from the Falkland Islands but I fear there is only one mail a month. – I am now going to see Captain Loftus Jones on board *Garnet* and shall find out all about my movements.

Dec 4th. – My sweet wife, I am in despair. We have to sail next Wednesday and I cannot hear of you before leaving. The telegraph is so expensive, that is until we get a code which Captain Bainbridge[4] will explain all about. He has kindly promised to see you and tell you all about my ship and the people in her, so when you receive this you will also get a letter from Mrs Bainbridge telling you when to expect them. It is a great comfort he has undertaken this, it will put you at ease I know. You should address your letters to H.M.S. *Dwarf*, Monte Video, South Coast of America, and they will be forwarded without fail when opportunity offers.

We shall return here in February and in the mean time rest assured you will hear from me by every opportunity. I find the steamer that calls in the Falklands is uncertain so you must be a brave little wife and not get anxious if you do not hear for some time.

We are going to the West Falklands in order to protect the seal fisheries. It appears that these fisheries are leased out by Government, but

[4] Captain Bainbridge was the previous captain of the *Dwarf* whom Wiseman was relieving. He was of commander's rank, but commanders were often addressed socially as captain.

the lessees find a number of American and other foreigners poaching to such an extent as almost to exterminate the seals. So they have petitioned the Government for protection, and the result is that we are to be sent down there. I should enjoy the trip were it not for the fact of not getting mails.

And now darling, to tell you something about the ship. She is in good order and clean. The officers seem a very pleasant and gentlemanly set. My cabin is very comfortable and has plenty of room. I wish I had brought out a few odds and ends from The Grange to put about, but perhaps you could pick out some little things from my smoke room. I need a blotting pad badly – how stupid of me not to bring one – but freight is very little and Whiteley would forward a box and save you all trouble. I hope you won't forget to send me a nice large photo of yourself. I want a very good one nicely done, and the chicks as well.

Now to tell you of my first day on board. After Divisions (when all the men and officers muster for inspection) we went to church on the lower deck. There is an harmonium on board which the Second Lieutenant Mr Luscombe plays very well. Some of the crew and officers form a choir and do excessively well I assure you, you would be very pleased with the Service. They sang from Hymns Ancient and Modern Nos 50, 463 and 269 – I shall try and get your favourites sung ere long, dear wife.

You will get this letter on about 5th January so I was right to send my Christmas and New Year's greetings to you by the last mail. I am beginning with this letter to number each, and will ask you to do the same as then we can tell whether all letters have arrived. Now sweet heart, I am going to compose our telegraph code...

As I write it is blowing a heavy pampero[5] and we are rolling and pitching about in a frantic manner, a nice welcome as I am taking up my abode and sleeping in my cabin for the first time. I have asked the First Lieutenant, Mr Seymour, to join me at dinner. The only thing in favour of this blowy weather is that it will detain us another day or two and I might get the longed-for letter from my dear wife. Capt Bainbridge will bring some photos and feather flowers and also some guava jelly for the chicks.

10 p.m. The wind has gone down and I am going to bed comforted. Mr Seymour dined with me tête-à-tête, and we had a long talk about the

---

[5] An infamous violent sou'wester that sweeps over the pampas of South America.

14

ship and all in her. I hope I shall be able to get you some seal skins from the Western Falklands. And now good night and God bless you.

Dec 5th. – A fine day after the blow, and I am going to be busy getting ready for our start south. – We have to coal, provision, and make all sorts of preparations. I have just returned from *Garnet* and find she goes off tomorrow in search of the Pacific Mail Steamer *Patagonia*, news having arrived that she has broken down. A boat left her on the 18th November off the coast of Patagonia with her main shaft broken, so she has been dodging about under sail ever since. I hope for the passengers' sakes she has not come to grief. I am to remain here till Friday...

H.M.S. *Dwarf*
Monte Video
Dec 7th

My darling wife,

How do you like the Dwarf paper? After all the excitement yesterday *Garnet* has not gone out; just as she was starting a German steamer came in with the news that *Patagonia* had repaired her shaft and was steaming on her way. It was blowing fearfully all yesterday, and a pretty wetting I got on board the Senior Officer's ship. In the afternoon Capt. Bainbridge landed with me, and then I sent him off to the *Trent* – how I longed to be off as well.

Now exactly as to my movements. We sail on Saturday next for the Falklands. *Garnet* comes down about the 10th January with our mails, and then I return here as Senior Officer. Captain Jones comes back in March, and I think soon afterwards I shall take him up the river for a trip which will be very pleasant. I do not yet know whether it will be up the Parana or Uruguay river.

Yesterday evening Capt Jones of *Garnet*, Lieut Law commanding *Firefly*, Mr Luscombe our Second Lieut, Major Cantley (of whom more anon) and Mr Grenfell (a most pleasant man who owns an estancia up the Uruguay river) dined with me to inaugurate my reign on board *Dwarf* and a very good dinner we had, though I says it as should not. The cook left by Capt Bainbridge is a good man and does his work well. Fresh strawberries, cherries and asparagus on the 6th December, what do you think of that, poor little frozen mortal? Now to return to Major Cantley, he belongs to the Royal Engineers and has just returned from

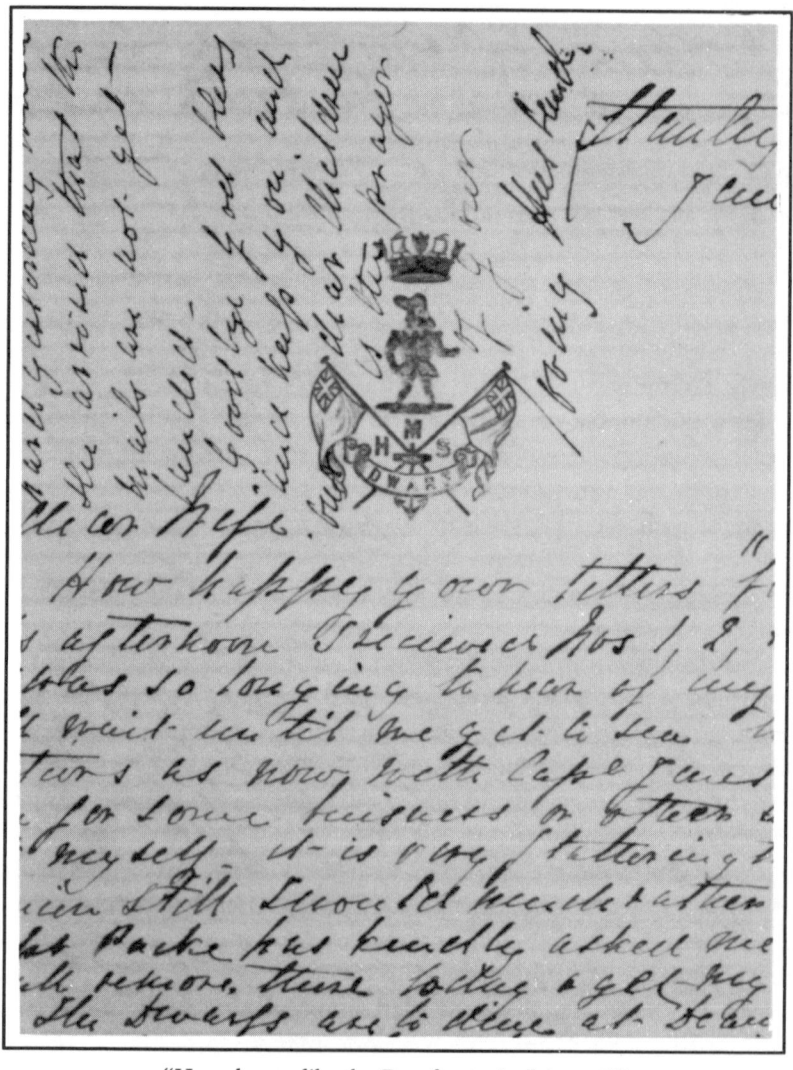

"How do you like the *Dwarf* paper?..." (page 15)

The curious letter-head of a curiously-named ship.

the Falkland Islands where he was sent to report on the necessary defences.

This morning *Garnet* has gone out to fire his quarterly allowance of ammunition but returns this evening.

Dec 8th. – Last evening I landed about five to pay my respects to the English Minister, the Hon. Mr Monson. He was not at home but met me afterwards at the Club and asked me to dine with him. Mrs Monson, a bride and very pretty, did the honours. Monson who is a middle-aged man has just married this young lady, who was a Miss Monroe, daughter of the late Consul-General. She is very pleasant and ladylike and plays well. After dinner some French Legation people came in and the captain of the French ship *Talisman*, the latter a great friend of Capt de Clare and a great admirer of madame. We had a very pleasant evening, and luckily it was a calm night so I did not get a ducking going off again to the ship.

I have left all my black satin neckties behind and had to buy a couple – will you send them?

I think we shall have a very interesting trip to the Falklands as we go to the West Island where hardly anyone has been except sealers and such like ruffians, and we may have to assert the authority of Britain by running in some of the Yankee gentlemen who have been poaching on the English fisheries. I hope I shall be able to get some skins.

Unfortunately here, as elsewhere, some letters or parts of letters are missing. But evidently after several delays Dwarf *left Montevideo bound for Stanley, and Sir William had a couple of fine days to rediscover his sea-legs.*

CHAPTER 2

ON PASSAGE TO THE FALKLAND ISLANDS

H.M.S. *Dwarf*
at Sea
Dec 12th 1881

Another lovely day. We are under sail and going along in perfect quiet with smooth sea and bright sunshine. It is most enjoyable, not a motion of any kind and perfect stillness. I only hope it may last, but feel we shall have a blow ere long as in these stormy regions we can hardly hope for such luck as a smooth passage throughout. This afternoon the wind dropped and we are once more under steam with a light southerly wind which blows very cold, quite like Scotland again. I got so cold that I went early to bed as the only place to get warm.

Dec 13th. – A pleasant breeze this morning and fair, so at halfpast eight I stopped steaming and once more under sail we had quiet. This ship is not a clipper. I thought *Lapwing* was dummy enough under sail but this ship is a thousand times worse. I do not think a gale would send her along more than about five miles an hour. I am tracing a chart for you of the Falklands so that you may be able to follow our journey in that part of the world. I will also copy from the South American Memoir what little of the history of those Islands is written as it may interest you now that *Dwarf* is going down there. The tracing is very untidy but I will do you a better one when I get an etching pen; this is only done with an ordinary steel pen so broad nibbed that I can do nothing but make blots all over the place.

Dec 14th. – I relaxed myself yesterday evening by playing a rubber of whist in the wardroom. All yesterday afternoon and through the night we had a fine fair wind and the ship to belie my prediction went seven knots for the greater part of the time, but on getting up this morning I found the barometer tumbling down as hard as it could and the wind inclined to draw to the west from north, so after prayers I close-reefed the topsails and reefed the foresail (there is a lot of nautical jargon for you to unravel) not before it was wanted, as the wind continued to freshen and draw ahead. At about half-past ten in the forenoon it was blowing a whole gale from the S.W. and is still a-going it. I am wedged in at my kneehole table with all the chairs and a few odd unbreakable things that have not been lashed flying about in the most annoying manner. This is one of the occasions qualified by Captain Corcoran of the *Pinafore*[6] as "what never, hardly ever!" This is a *hardly-ever* day – there goes another roll and lurch enough to drive one wild, though I am bound to say that the little ship is behaving very well indeed. Considering all things we might be worse off.

Dec 16th. – Last evening the wind went with the sun. The night was comfortable enough, and this morning Boreas[7] is at it again but not as hard as yesterday and we are able to make a few miles towards our desired haven. I only hope we shall not get another gale. Oh for a slant of fair wind! – another bit of nautical slang for my wife. The weather bar the windy part is lovely bright sunshine and a dry pleasant atmosphere. One of the engineers Mr Hawkins had to go on the sick list yesterday, on account of a desperate attack of sea-sickness. He is about this morning but looking very white about the gills. I fear he has come out of the list too soon as I doubt not we shall have another blow ere long. If we get along at all we shall be passing over the spot where the steamer *Patagonia* broke down, but although we have orders to look out for her I expect she has got on all safe by this time. I had asked some of the officers to dine last night but was obliged to put them off, and heaven only knows when I shall be able to have them as it would be only a discomfort for everyone in the present state of the weather. I shall be very glad when we get to the Falklands and still more when we get back to Monte Video.

Dec 16th. – We have been on our course all this morning but now at 11 a.m. this wind is heading a little. I exercised at gun drill for about half

---

[6] Sir William was a gifted amateur dramatist, and assisted W.S. Gilbert with the naval aspects of the writing and production of "H.M.S. *Pinafore*". In later life he wrote plays himself, and at least one was produced professionally in the West End. Captain Corcoran of H.M.S. *Pinafore* was "hardly ever" sick at sea.

[7] Strictly speaking Boreas was the god of the north wind, but here it is clearly a metonymy for damned awkward winds in general.

an hour but was obliged to secure as the sea began getting very rough again, and I feared we should have the big six-and-a-half-ton gun taking charge. The men seem to drill very well. Just a week out today and only 540 miles out of 1200 miles, what a dummy of a ship,[8] but I should not abuse my own ship should I? As long as she carries me safely and brings me soon home to my dear wife. If we do not get a slant of wind soon I fear we shall eat our Christmas dinner at sea instead of in Stanley Harbour.

Dec 17th. – A lovely day but no wind or at least very little. A barque passed us this morning bound for Valparaiso; she came up and passed us as if we had been anchored, looking very neat and pretty with all sail set. We had a little talk by signal and found out her name was the *Trinidad* from London 57 days out, which is not a bad passage as she has traversed about 7,000 miles of ocean. It is very annoying to be passed and left by a merchant ship but so the fates decree.

As the wind did not turn up, I started under steam about 6 p.m. and here we are. My proposed dinner party is to come off this evening. Mr Seymour, Webb, Hamm, and Horwill are the party asked.

Dec 18th. – Here we are at it again, blowing harder than ever from the S.W. with a very heavy sea, the ship spooning the water in over both sides, yours ever wedged in, "sitting tight" as Sir Henry would say. Trying to write this is as much as I can do in a very severe gale, and I fear it will last some time longer. But to go back to last night's doings. The dinner came off and was a great success. I find that both Hamm and Webb have been out in China and as this ship spent the first half of her commission on the west coast of Africa we all had much in common and consequently conversation did not flag at all. I like what I see of the officers very much. This morning about five a light westerly wind sprang up and pushed us along a bit. We saw our old friend *Trinidad* away to leeward and of course as we were under steam returned her compliment of yesterday by passing her. After divisions and my usual Sunday inspection to see that the men are clean and tidy and that every part of the ship

---

[8] Evidently there was some discussion on these lines with the Navigating Lieutenant, who has written in the ship's log for this date: "The ship sails very fairly indeed for one of her size with the wind well on the quarter and right aft, but of course owing to her being flat-bottomed, and having two screws, she is very leewardly the moment the wind comes on the beam."

"I like what I see of the officers very much..." (page 21)

Back row: Assistant Paymaster William Horwill, Assistant Engineer Hugh Hawkins, Boatswain Thomas Brenahan, unknown, Surgeon Maurice Mackenzie. *Front row*: Engineer Richard Hamm, Commander Sir William Wiseman, Lieutenant Montague Seymour, Lieutenant Fred Luscombe, Navigating Lieutenant George Webb.

They are all wearing frock coats, but otherwise there is a fair diversity of appearance. The captain is wearing his New Zealand medal which he gained in the Maori War of 1863–5. No one else wears a medal.

Photo: Wiseman Collection

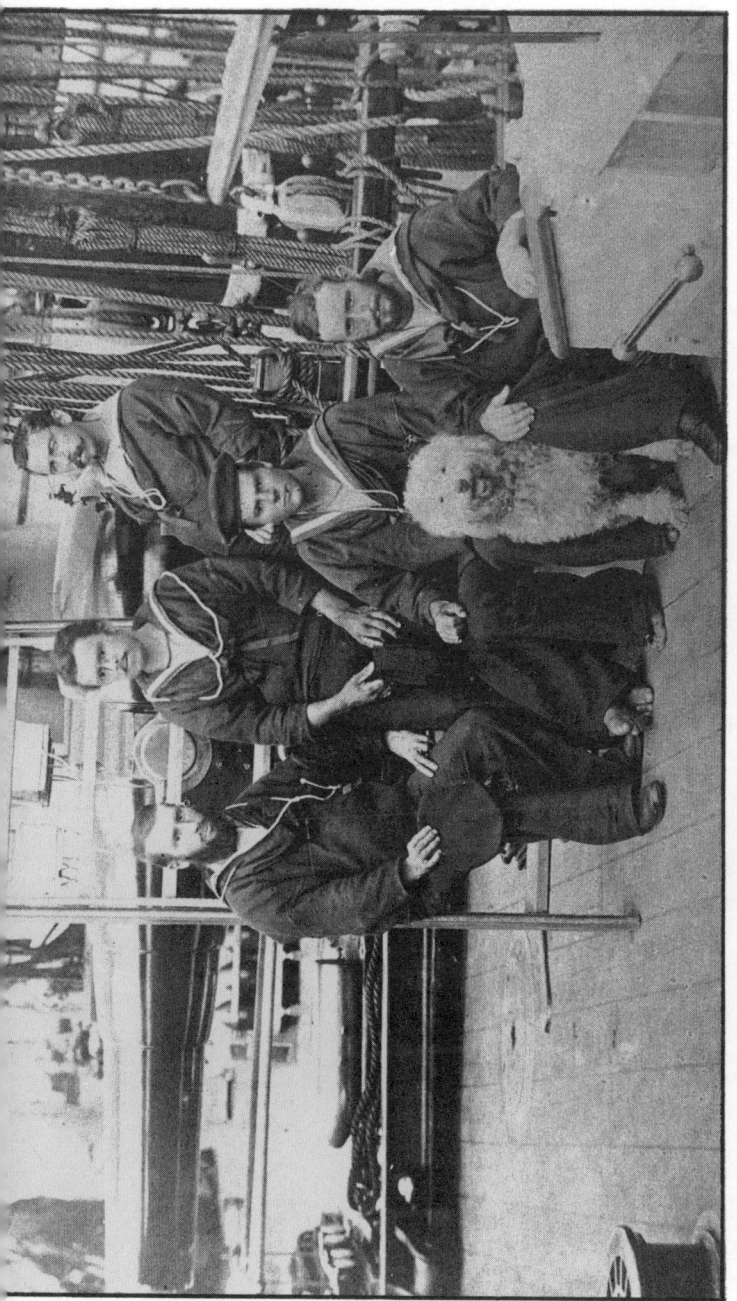

"The men are clean and tidy..." (page 21)

Some of the *Dwarf* ship's company are pictured here, possibly a gun's crew. Note the poodle and the bare feet. The *Dwarf*'s largest gun weighing 6½ tons is visible in the background, together with some of its 100-pound shells. The date on the trunnion is 1868. It is so highly polished that a vague reflection of the photographer is visible near the inboard end.

Photo: Wiseman Collection

is the same, we had Service on the lower deck; our hymns were nos. 231, 185, and 193 A and M. The wind was good enough to give us time to finish the Service, then on it came and it is now blowing like winking whatever that may be. I do hope it will moderate when the sun goes down, but as our Aberdeen friends would say "I hae me doots." If it does not I fear we shall spend our Christmas at sea and most probably in a gale of wind, which will not be cheering however seasonable.

Dec 19th. – The gale is over, but yesterday evening between six and eight it blew as I have never seen it before, and the seas were tremendous. Standing on our bridge which is ten feet above the upper deck you could see nothing but the enormous crest of a wave towering above you, and the next minute up we went high on the top of another roller. During the wind squalls, for it had become squally at that time, the force of the wind was extreme and we could hardly show any sail to it. The ship behaved very well and it was a capital trial for her as she will never see worse weather.

Today is simply lovely. After all the heavy clouds and flying scud of yesterday we have a bright sun, not a cloud in the sky, and such a bracing fresh feel about the air one cannot help feeling well. By the bye I forgot to tell you we saw the first albatross yesterday. He came sailing round the ship at the height of the gale and seemed to enjoy the whole thing amazingly. I could understand the Ancient Mariner shooting such an impudent bird, flying round the ship chaffing him, and generally behaving in an annoyingly cool manner when he is not in the best of tempers, what with the blow and being a little bilious on account of the ship knocking about. I do hope we shall get a little fine weather now but it seems very doubtful in these blowy regions.

Dear heart, you will doubtless wonder that I do not mention any book that I am reading. The fact is I find all my reading time at present occupied in studying the changes of orders and regulations connected with my profession, to say nothing of all the new drills, arms and weapons of destruction which have been introduced since last I was afloat. I am reading hard at them all and working away as if at school again.

Dec 20th. – We have a light fair wind this morning and our hopes with regard to a quiet Christmas are rising. It is getting very cold, thermometer down to 49 last night. I am going to get to work on my

Falkland Islands description today in case a mail is ready to start on our arrival.

Dec 21st. – The fair wind freshened yesterday afternoon and is now driving us along splendidly, blowing half a gale right aft. Even this old dummy cannot miss going. I do hope the fair wind will take us in to Stanley, we deserve it I am sure after all our knocking about. It is our only chance of having a quiet Christmas in harbour. I went to work at my Falklands account but am not quite satisfied with the result and intend having another go at it for correction.

My dear wife, even you would enjoy today's sail, the ship quite steady with every stitch of canvas set, flying along with no noise or engines to trouble.

11 p.m. We have had a splendid breeze all this afternoon, it freshened to a gale and blew us along finely. The worst of the business is it is thick and foggy which will not be pleasant for making the land, but I hope to find a clear day tomorrow. At any rate the ship can run on in safety until five o'clock in the morning when I must be up and doing, so good night, God bless you. I am writing this to the soul-stirring accompaniment of the fog-horn sounded every two and a half minutes. Do you remember the one at Aberdeen, because this is a smaller and more disagreeable version.

Dec 22nd. – Good morning at five a.m. We have had such a night of blowing, raining, thundering and lightening quite like the opening scene of Macbeth. – However we have got along and here is a fine bright morning with a good breeze to take us, I hope, into Stanley by the evening. As yesterday was the longest day in this part of the world it began early, the sun rising about 3.50 a.m. behind a bank of clouds which he gilded and painted in a most lovely manner (this reads rather like a plumber's sign-board, but never mind, you will understand me I know dear heart). Hooray, hooray, I think we shall have a quiet Christmas in harbour after all, geese for the shooting and mutton fourpence a pound, there's a place for you!

Later that day there was a heavy storm. The ship's log gives some idea of the complexities of seamanship required:
"9.20 Mustered by Divisions, read Prayers. Wind SW Force 8 to 10. Course SE half E. Speed [under sail] 8.2 knots. Watch employed

*variously. Carpenters stopping leaks on lower deck. 1 p.m. lit fires in 3
boilers. 1.30 p.m. Furled mainsail took in 2 reefs of Topsails. 2.00
Proceeded ahead with both engines slow speed. Trimmed sails as required.
Course ES half S. Speed 6 knots. Violent heavy squalls. Wind Force 6 to
10. 4.00 Land on Starbd beam. 4.20 shortened and furled sails. Down
top Glt yards, set foretrysail and inner jib. Pointed yards to wind... 7.25
Stopped and came to in 4 fms, veered to 2 shackles, out lower booms. Wind
WSW Force 8 to 9."*

Dec 23rd. – Oh, what a day we had yesterday. We arrived at Port
Stanley[9] where we are now comfortably at anchor, that is to say as
comfortably as we can be with a gale of wind blowing and constant hail
storms. Yesterday we made the land about one o'clock and ran along in
a perfect hurricane of wind and rain. Luckily it stilled sufficiently to
enable us to make the entrance of Stanley Harbour. I have marked on
your very untidy chart our track and the end of the red line is where we
are anchored.

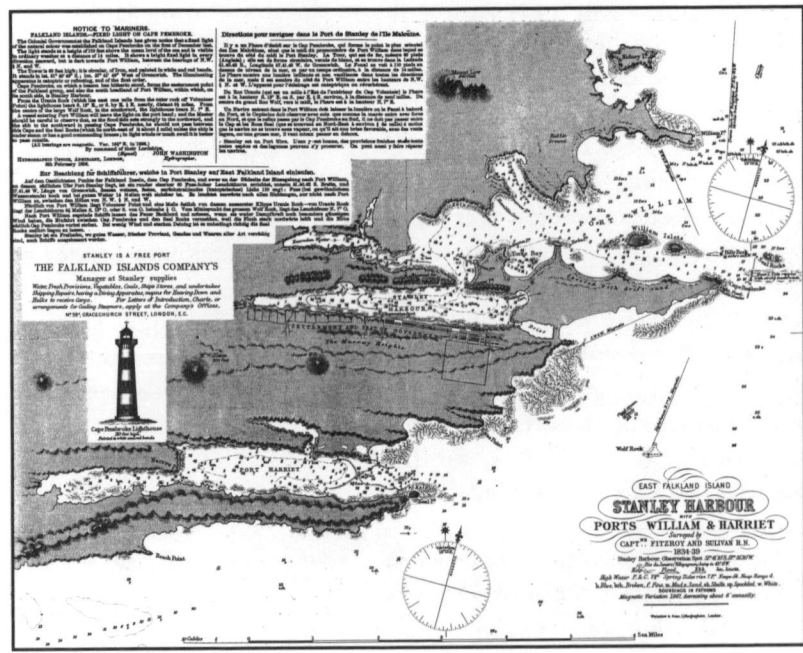

[9]See back endpaper.

26

"It stilled sufficiently to enable us to make the entrance of Stanley Harbour..." (page 26)

View looking south through the Narrows towards the town, at about the time of *Dwarf*'s visit.

Photo: Falkland Islands Company; Cobb Collection

27

Photo: Wiseman Collection

"Now comfortably at anchor, that is to say as comfortable as one can be with a gale of wind blowing..." (page 26)

This photograph shows a nasty squally wind blowing from different directions across the harbour, while storm clouds gather to the north. The three-masted barque at the end of the jetty is the *Dennis Brundrit* (see page 143).

Stanley Harbour

Another contemporary view of Port Stanley showing the harbour defences: three muzzle-loading field guns behind a rampart of peat, which makes a pleasant spot for a picnic on a fine summer's day.

Photo: Wiseman Collection

Showing the Flag

Harbour defences were useful as a last-ditch measure, but ultimately the security of British interests in the South Atlantic in the nineteenth century, as in 1914 and 1982, depended upon the Royal Navy. This photograph might stand as a paradigm for "Pax Britannica" – the navy quietly maintaining British interests around the globe, without fuss, without support, and often without specific instructions.

Here we see Stanley Harbour in February 1875 with what is probably the South Atlantic Flying Squadron (H.M.SHIPS *Narcissus, Immortalité, Topaze, Raleigh, Newcastle,* and *Doris*) lying at anchor, and the security of the Falklands assured.

Photo: William Biggs, from the collection of Miss Madge Biggs.

30

CHAPTER 3

PORT STANLEY FOR CHRISTMAS

H.M.S. *Dwarf*
Port Stanley
Falkland Islands
Dec 23rd 1881

I must send this off today as the mail sails in the afternoon, how lucky we caught her. I enclose a very shabby chart and the beginning of some scraps about this place which I will, like the penny horror, "continue in my next." I have to go and pay my respects to the Governor besides writing my despatch to the Senior Officer, so you must not mind if I finish abruptly. I shall get a flower and pop it in as my Christmas greeting.

Noon. I have just returned from calling upon Governor Kerr, he was of course very busy writing for the mail so I did not stay more than five minutes. He is a fine-looking old man with a long white beard, but as I dine tonight and meet Mrs Governor and the daughter you shall have a full description in my next budget. Now how can I describe Stanley? The nearest approach is if you can imagine Braemar with no trees or heather, all the larger houses taken away and instead of the Dee winding through a valley an arm of the sea coming right up to the moorland. Add to this a south west gale blowing night and day with intervals of heavy hail and rain squalls and you have Port Stanley as it appears to me. No doubt the inhabitants would repudiate this description but to me it seems a true one. To enhance the cheerfulness of the scene the harbour is full of dismasted ships that have come to grief on the passage round Cape Horn. However we must be thankful for small mercies, and no doubt will enjoy our Christmas dinner. I am having all the officers to dine with me to make our Christmas as home-like as possible, and I dine with the officers on New Year's Day. We shall sail next week, always supposing the gale is over, for the West Falklands, and go first to Bird

31

"A fine-looking old man with a long white beard..." (page 31)

Thomas Kerr C.M.G., Governor of the Falkland Islands 1880–1891.

Photo: Falkland Islands Government

"Now how can I describe Stanley?..." (page 31)

Ross Road looking west, taken at about the time of Wiseman's visit and showing the Italianate tower of Holy Trinity Church. The church was badly damaged in the peat slip of 1886 and subsequently demolished.

Photo: Collection of Mrs Eileen Jaffray

33

"The harbour is full of dismasted ships…" (page 31)

On the back of this photograph Sir William has written "Disabled ships. Duke of Argyle coming up Stanley Harbour." During the second half of the nineteenth century Stanley was in frequent use as a port of refuge for vessels damaged off Cape Horn. The Annual Report for 1881 records the arrival of twenty-nine ships, twenty-two of which "were in want of assistance or repairs, having met with disasters at sea. Two of them, the *Sussex* and the *Duke of Argyle* had been dismasted and had to remain in the harbour until new masts and rigging could be sent from England."

Photo: Wiseman Collection

"...that have come to grief on the passage round Cape Horn." (page 31)

The Finnish barque *Fennia* in Stanley after rounding the Horn, a graphic illustration of the kind of damage that was often incurred. The flourishing local trade in ship repair was accompanied by an equal interest in the salvage and insurance businesses, and decisions on sea-worthiness were not always made with an impartial eye. Dean Brothers and the Falkland Islands Company competed furiously for the larger share, keeping lookouts posted for ships in distress in order that their own agent should be first on the scene. Condemned vessels often ended their lives as storage hulks, as was the fate of the *Fennia*.

Photo: Falkland Islands Museum Collection

Island and then on to the Jason Islands making our head-quarters in Hope Harbour where there is plenty of shooting. I have marked the places in red ink on the chart.

God give you a bright New Year and may we be together again and enjoy our Christmas and New Year of 1882... Kisses to the chicks and love to mother.

Your loving husband.

P.S. I could only get some daisies growing by the road side, but these I send as my Christmas card.

Port Stanley

Falkland Islands

Dec 23rd

Was it not lucky dear wife,

The mail steamer which only calls here once a week sails today at two for Monte Video so I was enabled to despatch my No. 3 letter by her, and just after it had gone I found I had again forgotten your log, what an idiot I am but you must forgive me, I plead extreme blowy weather as an excuse. And when I tell you that ever since our arrival it has been blowing as hard as it was that day at home when all the trees at Barrington and Down Hall were blown down, and that as far as I can see it is likely to go on blowing in the same manner for an indefinite period, you must allow it is some slight excuse for me. Going up to Government House this morning I had to walk about a quarter of a mile, and it was quite as much as I could do to make headway against the wind; I should imagine the "cave of the winds" must really be situated somewhere in the Falkland Islands.

The very Act for making a close time for the seal fisheries, which we are sent down to enforce at the earnest request of the Governor, has not been passed yet. Can you imagine anything so stupid? We might just as well have waited for our mails at Monte Video. I shall give His Excellency a bit of my mind on the first quiet opportunity. I am so angry about it, fancy missing our mails for nothing. I must have shown my disgust at this stupidity for he said he would call his Legislative Assembly together as soon as possible and pass the law, but added he did not think he could get them together until three days after Christmas[10]. Whether they would take these three days to recover from the effects of their

[10] Legislative Council was actually convened, and passed the Bill, on 27th December.

36

"I had to walk about a quarter of a mile, and it was quite as much as I could do to make headway against the wind. . ." (page 36)

On his way to Government House in a westerly gale Wiseman would have battled past this row of terraced houses which included the Ship Hotel in the centre. With his theatrical connections he would have been intrigued if he could have known that ten years previously a girl had been born in the hotel to an actor and his wife who were visiting the Islands to try their hand at sheep-farming. Her name was Ellaline Terriss, and she was destined to take the Victorian stage by storm, marry Sir Seymour Hicks, and die in 1971 at the age of 100.

The Ship Hotel, now called the Upland Goose, is still one of the principal hotels in Stanley.

Photo: Falkland Islands Company

Christmas dinner or no I cannot say.

The Governor could not really be held to blame for this. He had transmitted a copy of the Ordinance for Colonial Office approval in June, and had waited for sanction until the last possible moment. Receiving no reply to his despatch, he was finally forced to proceed without the normal authorisation. He should perhaps, however, have realised sooner than he did that this lack of response from London might be connected with other mysterious anomalies becoming apparent in the machinery of Government. After Christmas his Colonial Secretary and Postmaster, John Wright Collins, was discovered to have secreted incoming dispatches in the back of his office drawers for many months. The story is continued by Wiseman later.

It is most amusing here, the Governor is every official rolled into one. The other day a man committed murder[11], well he was tried before the Governor as the only Judge in the place and sentenced, then it was discovered there was no one to hang him, so the Governor as Judge had to present a petition to himself as Governor begging for an annulment of the sentence. This the Judge in his capacity as Governor was graciously pleased to grant, and intimated his decision to himself in his judicial capacity. What do you think of that?

Sir William wrote elsewhere: "Whilst I was at Stanley the Governor's staff was rather reduced, consisting of the Governor's son who acted as Private Secretary to His Excellency, Secretary to the Legislative Council, Inspector of Prisons and Police, Harbourmaster and Clerk to the Supreme Court." A month later, after the Colonial Treasurer had "met with a severe accident" as described later, the Governor's son acquired in addition the duties of Colonial Secretary, Postmaster, Collector of Customs, and Shipping Master.

[11] This was the result of a quarrel between two seamen. John Gibson (alias Mark Charlton, according to the Deaths Register) a sailor from Nottingham, was murdered by fellow sailor Luke Johnson. Johnson had deserted from the British ship *Joseph* at Montevideo some months earlier and created problems by behaving "with considerable turbulence." He then shipped on the American whaler *Henry Trowbridge* which subsequently called at the Falklands, where the incident took place. His original death sentence was commuted to penal servitude for life by Executive Council on 10th March 1881, as they considered on representation that the circumstances amounted "to no more than an aggravated case of manslaughter."

By the bye I did not describe my reception at Government House. After struggling up against the wind in coat and sword I came to what I supposed was the front door, a glass door in a conservatory, but I found no means of ringing or knocking and as the door would not give I prospected round the house, and at the back found a door and what was equally important a knocker. With this I rat-tatted and at length a portly woman with a red face and glasses turned up, opened, and seemed so astonished to find someone in uniform that she fled to an adjoining scullery to turn her sleeves down and smooth her hair, after which operation she returned. I informed her that I wished to see Her Majesty's Representative, and was ushered through a lumber room into a large barn of a drawing room where I met His Excellency.

Dec 24th. – Christmas Eve, and a fine day, the wind having moderated considerably and the sun kindly consented to shine. Mackenzie the Doctor, Luscombe, Horwill and self set off for a shoot at ten o'clock attended by the faithful Minto (he is my coxswain). Off we started with flattering tales from the Doctor of the number of geese and snipe we should bring back, and away up the hills behind the settlement we trudged. The scenery was just like what we saw of the moors that day we went up with the Parkers from Aboyne, do you remember? Well, dismiss from the picture heather and woods and in their place imagine a short peaty grass, and you have the scenery here. Well, on we trudged but no snipe, however we killed a good many dotterel and hurried on to the creek where the geese were to be found, but what was our horror on gaining an overlooking ledge to see not a sign of a goose, nothing in the feathered line but an old gull, so we sat down to eat our lunch, after which we retraced our steps with only a dozen dotterel for our pains.

On regaining the settlement we met a gentleman who introduced himself as Mr Dean[12]. He is interested in the seal fisheries, and he introduced us to Mrs Dean. She seemed a pleasant woman and must have been good looking. Such a funny little house although it is one of

[12] George Markham Dean had arrived in the Falkland Islands in 1840 at the age of four, together with his parents and sister Frances. His father, John Markham Dean, acted as clerk and foreman to Mr Whitington, one of the first local entrepreneurs, but soon set up in business on his own account. By the time of Wiseman's visit J.M.Dean and Sons had become the most successful trading company in the Islands, and had also acquired farming interests on West Falkland at Pebble Island and Port Stephens, both of which *Dwarf* was later to visit.

"Going up to Government House this morning..." (page 36)

Government House today. The central stone portion of the building dates from the 1840s. Governor Kerr was in the process of constructing the wooden wing on the right at the time of Wiseman's visit.

Photo: Jane Cameron

"A glass door in a conservatory..." (page 39)

The Government House conservatories have justly been a matter of pride for many years. A visitor might still experience some confusion trying to find the correct entrance to the building.

Photo: Jane Cameron

41

"A large barn of a drawing room..." (page 39)

Governor Kerr had been christened "The Old Perisher" by West Falkland farmer Robert Blake, "referring perhaps to the chilly Government House drawing room in his day, where parties had been slow affairs" suggests Mary Trehearne in *Falkland Heritage*. An inventory of the furniture taken at the time lists among the contents "1 picture of H.M. The Queen". Comparison with this photograph of the drawing room today indicates that little has changed over the years, except the monarch in the picture frame.

Photo: Jane Cameron

the best here, all of the rooms low pitched so that you involuntarily stoop when entering into the drawing room, a conservatory with a good many English flowers, Pelargoniums, musk plant, roses, Canariensis, ferns of different sorts and in one corner a small holly tree to remind us of the season. In the garden outside daisies, both double and single, form all the borders, in fact the daisy seems the staple flower of this country, almost the only one I have seen in the open. Then in the kitchen garden some potatoes and a few peas trying hard to look as if they intended coming to maturity but feeling all the time they are a fraud.

We bade adieu to our host and embarked in the whaler on our way off to the *Dwarf*. I saw what I took to be two ducks swimming about, so telling the Doctor to load I gave chase. Bang goes the Doctor's gun and one victim falls, the other wounded, but we did not get him unfortunately so pulled back to the dead bird which proved to be a wild gosling in very good condition, this is another contribution to our Christmas dinner. And now after changing and having a cup of tea I am off to Government House to talk about seals.

Dec 25th. – A Merry Christmas and a Happy New Year, my dear wife. It is a lovely morning here, bright sunshine and calm weather, may it portend a happy future. I am busy this morning getting ready for Service at ten o'clock as the Colonial Chaplain asked me whether I should like his coming off to officiate. Of course I consented, and as his Service on shore is at eleven we had to hurry to be ready, but you shall have a faithful account of our doings later on.

We had Mr Brandon[13] the Chaplain and his wife and the two Miss Kerrs off to Church. The parson was not particularly eloquent and preached an extempore sermon of a very insipid character but the Service went off very well. The singing was really good and quite surprised the shore people. In the afternoon I put on an old suit and went for a

---

[13] The Rev. Lowther E. Brandon was Colonial Chaplain in the Falkland Islands for thirty years. Arriving in 1877, he was appointed Dean on the consecration of the Cathedral in 1892, and continued to serve until 1907. Immensely energetic, he founded and edited the Falkland Islands Magazine, effectively the first newspaper, started a temperance society, was for many years Inspector of Schools, and ran a children's library and savings bank. In addition to these activities, he was well-known for his indefatigable travels in camp, spending many hours on horseback visiting remote houses, accompanied always by his famous magic lantern, which he used to educate and entertain.

"Such a funny little house..." (page 39)

Photo: Falkland Islands Museum Collection

Stanley Cottage, also known for many years as Mrs Dean's Cottage, was one of the earliest houses in the town, having been built in 1844 by Henry Joseph Hamblin, the first Colonial Surgeon, as his own residence. George Markham Dean bought the house in 1866, and his widow continued to live there for many years after his death in 1888. Today Stanley Cottage houses the offices of the Education Department.

44

long walk with the doctor, about fourteen miles and then got on board to be ready for my guests.

The Dwarf's Second Lieutenant, Frederick Luscombe, was keeping a journal during this cruise. He wrote "Xmas day the parson came on board, and performed Divine Service. The Miss Kerrs accompanied him: we sang the same old Xmas hymns and it was such a fine day we had church on the upper deck. After dinner at noon all the men went ashore until the next morning, a capital riddance, as they had had plenty of beer, and were rather noisy. We all dined with the captain in the evening, Captain Packe as well."

Dec 26th. – The dinner was a great success you will be glad to hear. Besides the officers, Captain Packe[14] a large sheep owner came off to dine, he had asked me to join him at Christmas dinner but as my party was made up he came to me instead. We had a very jolly evening. I found out that Capt. Packe was cousin to the Harmonds who were at school with me in Switzerland, the Dowager will remember them well. Dear wife, you will think we are very dissipated in the Falklands. I am off on a shooting expedition today, and this evening there is to be a concert at the Government Stores given by the Governor to the people of Stanley, so I shall say goodbye until tomorrow morning.

Dec 27th. – I have survived the day, but to begin. The shooting party consisting of Luscombe, Horwill, the Doctor, young Kerr the Governor's son and your husband started off in a small two-ton yacht belonging to Mr Bailey[15] the police commissioner for Sparrow Cove[16] to get hares and geese. Off we went with a fair wind, and in an hour landed in the cove; this landing was a most perilous matter as the yacht's dinghy

[14] Captain R.C.Packe was one of the pioneering sheep-farmers of the Falklands, having first taken up land in 1847. He leased large areas of land, mainly around Stanley to begin with, but was later joined by his brother Edward, and together they established farms on West Falkland. The family left the Islands about the time of the Second World War, but continued to own land on West Falkland until the 1980s.

[15] Arthur Bailey had been in the Islands for over thirty years, having arrived as Surveyor-General in 1848. The post was abolished in 1873, but he continued to serve the colony as Registrar General, Receiver of Wrecks, Police Magistrate and Coroner until his death in 1883.

[16] See back endpaper.

was only the size of a decent washing tub and we could only go two at a time. However after a little time we mustered our forces and spread out to beat up the hares. I should tell you that for beaters we had my coxswain and a pilot who brought the cutter round. He is an extraordinary character, an old sealer having been twenty-five years at that trade and not made anything, all his money having gone in drink. Ten years ago he turned over a new leaf, cut the sealing trade and whisky, turned his attention to teetotalling and running a posting schooner round the islands, and is now doing well[17].

Off we set, two of our men bringing up the rear with lunch etc. We started a good many hares, but like ours near the Grange they were very wild and bolted a long way out of shot, but we got a few dotterel. After walking for about an hour we got to the crest of a hill and looking over to the next crest I saw what appeared to be a number of blocks of chalk stuck up in a row, but on looking closer I found they moved and that there was black about them. It dawned on me that these must be penguins and so disposed to be a flock at their rookery. What absurd birds, all standing in rows looking like fat old gentlemen with large white waistcoats and very short arms! On getting up to their nests, which look like half finished rooks' nests built on the ground, the birds waddled round us hissing and snapping while we examined the eggs; a great many were just hatching and some of the little fellows out, just like young ducks all black and white down. We cut off one old bird and having thrown a strap round him under his flappers inspected him closely. They certainly are the most curious birds I ever saw. They can hardly be said to be feathered, their covering being more like seal skin and their flappers covered with hard scales, white breasts and black head and backs, waddling about in flocks looking like a procession of fat well-to-do City men. I got one of their eggs and got it blown.

On we went after looking at the penguins and soon saw some grey dots on the grass down by the sea; these we knew to be geese and divided our forces. I went off to the left where a pond was situated, thinking they would make for that after being disturbed, and the others lined the ground and walked up the birds. On the way round to the pond I shot a kelp goose, a pure white bird with the most beautiful

[17] Probably William Ratcliff, who captained the coastal schooner *Orissa* for some time.

"They certainly are the most curious birds..." (page 46)

The Gentoo (*Pygoscelis papua*) is one of the three common species of Falkland Islands breeding penguins, the other two being the Rockhopper (*Eudyptes chrysocome*) and the Magellanic, or Jackass as it is locally known (*Spheniscus magellanicus*). Each species has its own distinctive appearance and behaviour patterns. This young gentoo is in the process of losing its infant down, revealing the short, oily feathers of the adult bird. As in Wiseman's day, penguins are still numerous in the Islands, and continue to be remarkably unafraid of man.

Photo: Jane Cameron

down under his feathers. They are not good eating but the skins are such as ladies do admire, and I shall try and get one lady some of them. After getting to my station I heard two or three shots, and over came a large flock of geese, the ordinary wild goose and some of the finely marked brent geese. They alighted some hundred yards from where I had posted myself, and as there were no bushes or other cover I tried to crawl up near them on all fours but did not succeed in getting nearer than twenty yards which was rather far for No.4 shot. So I only succeeded in driving them back to the others, who got another broadside at them. I then walked up to the head of the pond and shot a couple of teal.

After lunch we pressed a government horse into our service for carrying home the game which amounted to eleven geese, a brace of teal, some dotterel and my kelp goose. This horse fell victim to his partiality for bread and was captured with the aid of a small piece, when with the aid of two knife-lanyards we extemporized a bridle and loaded him with our spoil. We started early as we had to be back for the concert, an account of which I will give you later on, and after a pleasant sail arrived once more back on board the *Dwarf*.

Dec 27th. – To tell you all about the concert: it was held in the Government Store House, a large room very prettily decorated with flags, a raised platform at the far end for the performers, and rows of benches made of deck planks supported by empty spirit demijohns. I enclose a programme to which there was an addition of two songs by Seymour the 1st Lieut. who accompanied himself on the guitar; these songs were really the success of the evening and were both encored when he gave fresh songs.

And now to explain who the performers were: first on the pro-gramme, Mrs Brandon, she you have already heard of as coming off with her husband the Chaplain for Service on Christmas day, she is a bride, very plain, most energetic in getting up reading clubs, mothers' meetings etc. She plays well and accompanied all the evening. I should be inclined to think she had been very much soured in early life, perhaps poor thing she has been a governess.

Miss J. Williams is the daughter of a solicitor who, not finding the good people of Cheltenham sufficiently litigious, came out here to try sheep farming. Rumour in the shape of young Kerr the Governor's son says he came out with nothing and now pays an interest of £1500 a year

"We pressed a Government horse into our service for carrying home the game..." (page 48)

Wiseman and his party were doing what most Islanders would have done in the same situation. Until the 1950s, horses were the principal mode of transport, both for people and freight, across "camp", the term used to describe all land outside Stanley. This photograph was taken at Fitzroy in 1938 by a visiting agronomist.

Photo: William Davies. Falkland Islands Museum Collection

on his debts. He is a hypochondriac and never leaves the house. The daughters sing very fairly and got through the Elfin Call very well. They are not beauties, but great hulking girls with red and white faces and light hair.

Mr Cobb is agent to the Falkland Islands Company which owns the greater part of the East Island, with sheep and cattle farming. His stock in trade is a very fair baritone voice and he sang Mary Lee well. He has the only brick house in Port Stanley, and a very comfortable one it is with a good billiard room. It is not a handsome house, looking exactly as if some giant had picked up a detached villa from Brixton or Putney and popped it down in the Falkland Islands. His wife looks old enough to be his mother but seems pleasant.

Now for the Governor's family. First His Excellency is a very pleasant, gentlemanly man, most unsophisticated as indeed are all his family. He has lived nearly all his life in the West Indies principally at Barbados. Mrs Kerr is a very pleasant motherly creature who has never been to England in her life, having been born in the West Indies and always lived there. The elder Miss Kerr is certainly good looking, à la Mrs Langtry, and they are both nice ladylike girls. The son has been studying law in England and seems a good boy but very delicate suffering from heart.

And now that I have given you an outline of characters engaged in singing I will say a word about the audience. I was given the seat of honour in the centre supported by Mrs Cobb on one side and Mr Bailey the police magistrate on the other. Then the principal inhabitants and the officers off the ship filled the first two rows, and the whole population of Port Stanley, or the greater portion, filled the remainder of the room. Whole families came just as they used at our Clyde balls, babies and all, a most good-natured audience who consumed terrible quantities of tea and cake during the interval. The whole thing was given by the Governor to the inhabitants as a Christmas treat and they responded to his invitation well, three hundred and fifty (not including babies) coming out of five hundred souls.

After the concert I went up to Government House and supped with the Kerrs and then off to bed. Today I lunched at Government House and returned calls on Mrs Cobb, Mrs Dean, Mrs Brandon and Capt. Packe. At the latter's house I dine and sleep tonight. By the bye His Excellency was actually able to get his Council together today and they

"Mr Cobb is agent to the Falkland Islands Company…" (page 50)

This energetic Colonial Manager for the Falkland Islands Company came to the Islands in 1867 at the age of nineteen, and remained until 1891, when he returned to London to run the Company's offices there until his retirement as Chairman in 1922. He was a keen amateur photographer and meteorologist. This photograph was taken in Stanley House in the 1880s.

Photo: Falkland Islands Company

51

"A detached villa from Brixton or Putney…"(page 50)

Stanley House, built in 1878 by the Falkland Islands Company, as a home for their Colonial Manager. As Wiseman notes, it was at the time the only brick house in Stanley, and brick buildings have remained scarce, due to the expense of importing the materials, although ships occasionally used bricks as ballast. The two other buildings clearly visible in the photograph conform to the more normal pattern of construction, being timber framed with weatherboard cladding. Ship's timbers often ended their days incorporated into such structures, as the spars supporting the buildings on the left show.

Other points of interest in the photograph include the casks and spars littering the foreshore, and the flagstaff at the top of the hill at left. This was used for signalling the lighthouse on Cape Pembroke, seven miles distant, and also as a lookout post, especially by the small boys employed as runners for the shipping agents to bring early news of the approach of vessels in distress. The object at centre left which appears to be a diving board is part of F.E. Cobb's meteorological apparatus, a platform for his aeronometer to measure wind speed.

Photo: Falkland Islands Museum Collection

52

Ethel Cobb, daughter of F.E. Cobb, in the garden of Stanley House with her pet owl "Jenny". This is a short-eared owl (*Asio flammeus sanfordi*); the species breeds in the Falklands although it is not common. The original lantern slide from which this print is taken has a note on it saying that the owl was "caught with broken wing near Stanley and taken home to zoo in London". The tradition of speaking of Britain as "home", which began naturally enough with the early settlers, persists to this day, even among islanders who have never been to Britain, although most still have relatives there.

Photo: Falkland Islands Company; Cobb Collection.

53

passed the Close Season bill[18].

Dec 28th. – I had a very pleasant evening at Packe's and an excellent dinner. He has a French woman cook who does things well. I heard all about Miss Jervis (the young lady whom Mr Calverly, Sir Henry's nephew, is engaged to). Packe who is a Norfolk man and knows her people says she is very pleasant and nice, but that the father is an awful old party, very wealthy, the only drawback being that are a number of children.

This morning it is blowing and hailing in squalls. I do hope it will drop by the evening as I want to get off tomorrow, first to Lively Island where there is good shooting, then to George Island, then to Bird Island to look after the seals, and after that to the Jasons calling at some of the Western ports, then down through Falkland Sound and back here by the end of January. I shall leave this letter behind me to go by the mail leaving here on the 18th January, and we shall go up to Monte Video with the first February mail. I hope to meet the *Garnet* in the course of the next fortnight and get our mails. How I long for a letter and news of my dear wife!

I enclose a piece of lichen picked off the rock close to the penguin rookery. Is it not a beautiful colour? I came off here after breakfast and in the forenoon had a visit from the American Consul, a most objectionable Yankee with an awful twang. This evening I dine at Mr Cobbs and sleep again at Capn. Packe's. On second thoughts I shall take this letter with me as far as Lively Island, as Mr Cobb goes with me so far and can take it back again in time for the mail.

Dec 29th. – I landed at four yesterday afternoon, and went up to Government House with Seymour and the Doctor for afternoon tea, and then to Capn. Packe's to dress for dinner. My host was dining at Cobb's also, and we walked down together. The party at Cobb's consisted of Mrs Cobb[19], a sister of hers a Miss Blake, the master of the

---

[18] This bill made it illegal to hunt seals between 1st October and 1st April. Large fines were prescribed, of which half was to be paid to the person who gave the evidence.

[19] Emily Cobb was the sister of Robert Blake. She had married Frederick Cobb in 1873, and when they left England for the Falklands they were accompanied by Robert, somewhat at a loss for a career. Cobb arranged for him to gain some farming experience with the Falkland Islands Company at Darwin. After a short time Blake went into partnership with Ernest Holmested at Shallow Bay, and later established his settlement at Hill Cove.

house, and a Dr Hewson[20] from Darwin settlement besides Packe and myself. It was a very dull dinner, the ladies having simply nothing to say and the men not much, so we got away about ten o'clock and after a smoke went to bed.

I was up this morning at seven and after seeing my traps packed went off to Government House to get the official copy of the Seal Fishery Act and bid goodbye to the good folks there. I breakfasted with them, and after considerable delay got off. The old Governor is a charming man but such a fuddler and very loath to lose anyone to whom he can pour out his troubles, and they are many. His Treasurer, a Mr Collins, who came to the colony as a schoolmaster has been gradually made Harbour Master, Treasurer, Clerk of the Council, Postmaster and Colonial Secretary all in one for the very munificent salary of two hundred a year. He has been suppressing registered letters, despatches etc. and misappropriating public funds, at least the latter is the surmise. So the Governor asked me to let the ship's Paymaster go into his accounts which were all in disorder to discover what had been done, and a pretty state of things is disclosed, but the Governor is so good-hearted he wants to let this man off which would be utterly useless as he is a drunkard too. I fear the Governor will get a rap over the knuckles from home it he does not take action about Mr Collins.

Sir William wrote elsewhere: "(This official) combined the duties of Colonial Secretary and Postmaster General. He met with a severe accident shortly after my arrival, which confined him to jail with hard labour for several years. This unfortunate gentlemen had a passion for collecting coins and stamps. The former he obtained by opening letters at the Post Office and abstracting any remittance they might contain, whilst so eager was he to obtain specimens of the latter that he did not wait until the stamps had been used, but took several hundred pounds' worth from the Colonial Chest."

The Paymaster's report dated 29 December 1881 detailed a number of "grave errors" in the accounts, which it seems the Governor felt he could not ignore. Collins was therefore "apprehended". The Police Magistrate forced open a locked cupboard in his office, and a wealth of incriminating evidence

---

[20] Dr. B. Tydd Heuston had been the Assistant Colonial Surgeon, based at Darwin, since 1879.

fell out. Collins, among other fraudulent schemes, had been selling the
highly-prized Falklands stamps to collectors in England and pocketing the
proceeds.

Collins was tried on several charges by the Falkland Supreme Court, the
Governor presiding as judge. He pleaded guilty, was given seven years'
penal servitude, and was sent to Malta to serve his sentence, as the
Falklands had no facilities for long term prisoners.

Collins was actually sentenced on 13 January 1882, which means that
the whole of this complex case was completed in just nine working days.

A curious incident happened yesterday. In the afternoon a three-masted schooner[21] put in, having been severely damaged in that gale we encountered a week ago. She was on her way to the west coast of South America and was damaged off Staten Island and had to put back to the Falkland Islands. The curious part of all this is that her Captain is the brother to one of our engine room artificers and so they met in this unexpected way.

His Excellency came on board to say goodbye and brought some lovely flowers from the ladies, I can tell you some of their names – primulas, pansies, musk, geranium, wallflowers, mignonette, these are the principal ones, all grown in conservatories. After mutual adieus and the arrival of Mr Cobb who goes down with us as far as Choiseul Sound, and on whose island (Lively Is. by name) we are to shoot hares tomorrow, I started with fine weather and here we are half way to our destination with smooth sea and bright sky.

[21] This was the British schooner *Bride*, bound for Valparaiso with a cargo of coal. Her bulwarks had been carried away in a storm off Staten Island, near the coast of Tierra del Fuego.

CHAPTER 4

LIVELY ISLAND, DARWIN, MOTLEY ISLAND

Dec 30th. – We arrived last night in Choiseul Sound[22] and anchored in East Cove at eight o'clock.

The seaweed called kelp is most remarkable round these islands, growing as it does on rocks some twelve or even twenty feet under water. Spreading to the surface it marks perfectly all dangers and at the same time breaks all the sea, having the appearance of a patch of oil in the troubled waters. Our harbour was simply perfect, an entrance about one hundred yards wide led to a land-locked basin with smooth water.[23] On the outer peninsula we saw some guanacos,[24] the first time I have ever seen these animals alive; do you remember the rug Dr Humphry lent us for sleighing was made of their skins?

This morning at daylight I got under way and ran over to Lively Island where we met two of Cobb's brothers who are sheep farming. We landed in force, five guns, Mr Seymour, Luscombe, Dr Mackenzie, Horwill and myself to shoot hares on Phillimore Island which is just opposite. What a day we have had, blowing and raining all the time, but we succeeded in bagging thirty hares and seven couple of snipe, so that is not bad. We had tremendous walking and got very wet but altogether voted it a good day.

I went to the Cobb's ranchio[25] where they live and was ushered into a small room with a cooking stove in one corner, a table in the other, two or three wooden chairs and a deal table. Above was an attic with two beds and beyond a sanctum with a few pictures, indifferent water colours

[22] For the ship's track around the Falkland Islands see front endpaper.
[23] This is the present naval harbour.
[24] These animals closely resemble llamas, and their correct identification is *Lama guanicoe*, of the family *Camelidae*. They are not native to the Falklands, having been imported from the South American mainland about 1862.
[25] Wiseman's invented word seems to mean a ranch-house for an estanciero (land-owning farmer). Rather apt.

"We saw some guanacos..." (page 57)

Guanacos (*Lama guanicoe*) were introduced to the Falklands from the South American mainland in about the 1860s, probably because of the commercial potential of their fine wool. However they never really became established, and although another attempt was made in the 1930s, only a few hundred exist today, on Staats Island, where these were photographed.

Photo: Tony Chater

58

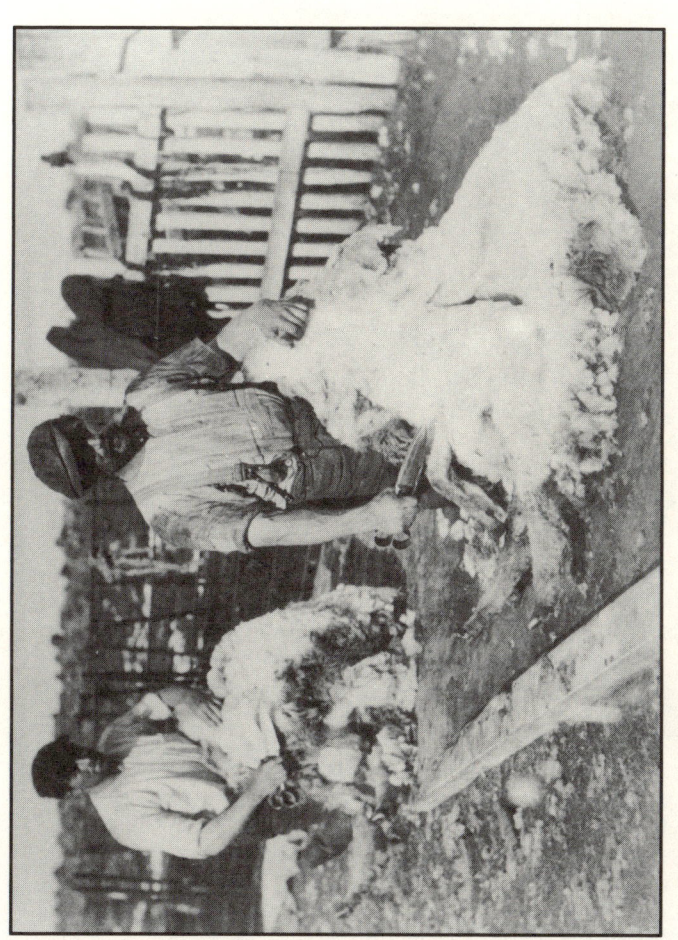

" ...to Lively Island where we met two of Cobb's brothers who are sheep farming." (page 57)

This photograph of shearers on Lively Island shows some of the reality of working life on the smaller farms. F.E. Cobb's brothers, H. and G. Cobb, leased Lively, and his son Arthur ran Bleaker Island.

Photo: Falkland Islands Company; Cobb Collection.

Shearing gang

The brand on the bales is "AFC" (Arthur Frederick Cobb, son of F.E. Cobb) which probably means that this photograph was taken on Bleaker Island.

Photo: Falkland Islands Company; Cobb Collection

60

and some books, standard authors in prose and verse. Over the fireplace was a large pipe-rack and against the wall saddles and other requisites. A most rough-looking house.

After all these explorations we returned on board and I dined in the wardroom where I am writing at midnight with a most bothering gale blowing so hard that I hardly like to go to bed.

Dec 31st. – The last day of the year. May the coming year bring you peace and happiness and may we soon be together again in our home and perhaps ere long a real home of our own. Dear wife, I cannot say I shall think of you more today than on other days for I do not think it is possible, may God bless you.

I am going up Choiseul Sound as far as Darwin to spend New Year's Day. It is the head-quarters of the Falkland Islands Company, so our Mr Cobb the manager is to show us round the bullock corrals – I say "our Mr Cobb" in contra-distinction to the brothers who farm Lively Island.

I have been looking over what I wrote last night and fear you will have some difficulty in deciphering it, but I was tired and rather anxious about the ship so you must excuse short-comings. I did not get to bed until nearly two o'clock and was called at four, so even now I am not very bright.

I should have described our walk yesterday better. It was most interesting. The island is covered with grass called tussac, which is a gigantic sedgy grass; the average length of the blade is 7 feet and of the stalk 4 to 6 feet. The plant grows in bunches closely together, and as many as 250 roots spring up from one bunch. In old plants the decayed roots of successive shoots form a cushion of dry entangled fibres which rise 7 feet and 6 feet in diameter, so that a person standing in a patch of old tussac may be quite sheltered or concealed. It grows with great luxuriance on the coasts, down to high water mark; and cattle and horses feed on it with the greatest avidity, and speedily become fat. About 3 or 4 inches of the roots are very agreeable to man, being crisp and of a nutty flavour. It was the food of two Americans who were upon the Western Island for fourteen months. The grass growing in large tufts upon the high base of decayed roots resembles a diminutive grove of thickly clustered palms; and from the dark green and luxuriant appearance given to the smaller islands clothed with tussac the richness of tropical vegetation is forcibly brought to memory. So says Mr Finlay in his Sailing Directory, and I am

"A sanctum with a few pictures..." (page 57)

Photo: Falkland Islands Company; Cobb Collection

This photograph illustrates well the kind of surroundings in which most Falkland Islands farmers lived in the 1880s. The small rooms of the simple timber-framed buildings were made as comfortable as possible, but luxuries were scarce. Note the roughly-made cupboard with the gun propped against it, the small shelf of books, the family photographs, and the watercolours of English scenes. The newspapers covering the table, still with their folds visible, indicate the recent arrival of a mail from "home". On the cupboard stands a box camera, evidence of the Cobb's long standing enthusiasm for photography.

"Mr Cobb the manager is to shew us round the bullock corrals..." (page 61)

By the 1880s the Falkland Islands Company was in a transitional stage between cattle ranching, which had once been the Company's main activity, and sheep farming, which was fast becoming the staple industry of the Islands. This stone corral at Darwin was built in 1874.

Photo: Spruce

63

"Tussac is a gigantic sedgy grass..." (page 61)

Tussac grass (*Parodiochloa flabellata*) once fringed much of the Falklands coastline, but uncontrolled grazing and fires seriously depleted stands over the years. Highly valued as animal fodder, it is now found most plentifully on offshore islands, but it is also becoming re-established in protected mainland areas, where its importance as a wildlife habitat is widely recognised.

This photograph was taken by Gustav Schulz, a German photographer who produced an album of pictures taken of the Falkland Islands in 1889.

Photo: Falkland Islands Museum; Schulz Collection

64

bound to say, bar the anecdote about the Americans which I can hardly swallow although the root is just what he describes it, his description is accurate.

The story of the marooned Americans subsisting for fourteen months on West Falkland is in fact true, although it must be said that their diet consisted of more than just tussac. They were found in 1842 by H.M.S. Sparrow, *which was exploring the islands with Governor Moody on board. They were examined by the captain of the* Sparrow, *Lieutenant John Tyssen, who wrote this report:*

"Henry Whiteman native of Great Britain, aged 18 years, and Samuel Profit, native of New Providence, U.S., aged 24 years state: That on the 18th or 28th December 1840, they left the American brigantine Enterprise, *John Green master, in company with another seaman named John Bray; that, to the best of their knowledge, they landed with the brigantine's dinghy in Queen Charlotte's Sound, West Falkland; that the cause of their leaving the brigantine was discontent at their treatment; that John Bray, after various disagreements amongst themselves, separated from them about two and a half months after their landing; that they subsisted on the wild fowl of the island, seals, roots of the tussac (daily), and the berries of the heather[26]; that they were healthy and did not experience any very severe weather (in comparison with the winters in the United States); that, with the exception of two days, they ate their victuals raw, being unable to procure fire; that at times they were attacked by the warrahs or foxes, and killed 12 of them.*

"When they were brought on board H.M. KETCH Sparrow, *at White Rock Harbour, they were in a good state of health, but from the middle downwards were without clothing, and the upper parts were barely covered with rags."*

The tussac on Phillimore Island is however very young and not much larger than long grass at home except at the two extreme points where there is a great quantity of the old dead plant in high tufts.

I was astonished in putting my foot down on one of these tufts to hear

---

[26] Presumably this is diddle-dee (*Empetrum rubrum*) which is common all over the Falklands. Similar to heather in appearance, it is covered with red berries in summer which have a refreshing, if somewhat astringent, taste.

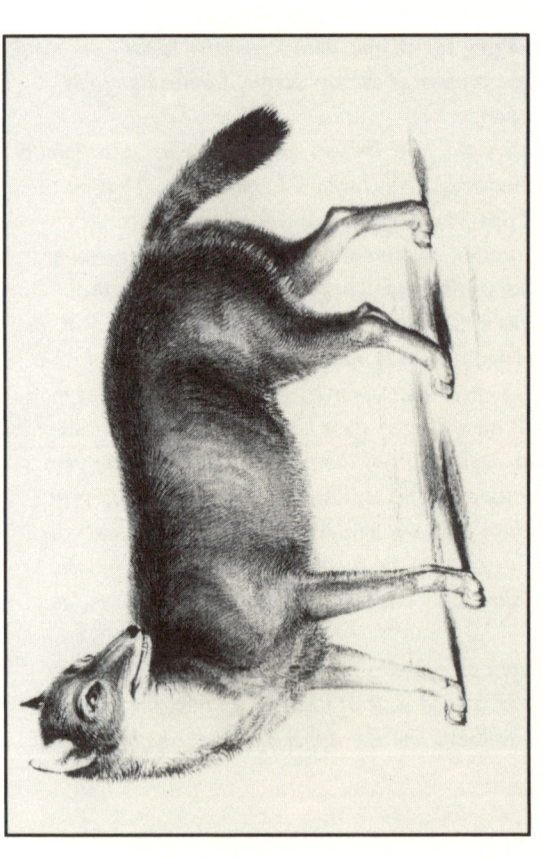

"At times they were attacked by warrahs or foxes..." (page 65)

It is highly unlikely that anyone was attacked by a warrah, the antarctic fox or wolf *Dusicyon australis*, whose chief characteristic was its extreme tameness. It seems much more probable that the warrah's natural curiosity and lack of fear made it approach the two men, who mistook a friendly overture for a threat. The warrah was a handsome creature, unique to the Falkland Islands, and its history and sources of food are still obscure. The early sheep farmers believed warrahs threatened their flocks, and systematically slaughtered them. Their friendliness made this very easy, and the last one is believed to have been shot in 1876.

Darwin was extremely interested in the warrah. This fine picture comes from his *Zoology of the Voyage of the Beagle*. It was probably painted by Augustus Earle, the *Beagle's* official artist and draughtsman. Darwin was a poor artist, knew it, and regretted it.

This warrah looks lively and alert, but in fact has been dead for 133 years. She is one of only two mounted specimens in existence, and was tracked down to the Institut Royal des Sciences Naturelles in Brussels by Kit and Katharine Layman in 1990, and generously lent by the Institut to the Falkland Islands Museum.

Photo: Jane Cameron

a most unearthly sound, something between a hiss and a croak, proceeding apparently from the root itself. On looking closely I saw first a long black bill and then the head of a penguin coming out of a hole at the root. I afterwards noticed hundreds of these birds in roots of tussac. It appears they make these old dead stumps their homes while on shore, burrowing like rabbits but to no great depth. -

All the sea-birds are bringing up their young just now, and whilst walking by the beach you may see twenty different species of ducks and geese, the old birds taking care of their little ones and teaching the little down-covered animals to paddle to the edge of the water. I saw kelp geese, brent geese, the ordinary wild geese, and loggerhead ducks, a most peculiar species whose wings never develop sufficiently to admit of their flying although when seen in the water they appear full-feathered. Then there were teal of different sorts, and in the centre of the island I saw a bird somewhat resembling the sandpiper, with the little chicks looking just like young partridges. So you may well fancy how interesting our afternoon was apart from the sport and how much I wished to have shown all these interesting things to my wife.

I should have told you that the Cobb brothers have a dairy farm on Lively and that one of them attends and milks their six cows every day. We all dined in the wardroom and the farmer brothers slept on board. This morning during a lull I put them on shore for it is still blowing hard, and at one o'clock D.V. we start for Darwin.

Midnight. – Many, many happy new years for my dear wife. We started at one o'clock and after a somewhat stormy passage arrived here by half past five. We had some heavy hail and snow storms to remind us of what the weather was at home. Mr Cobb and self dined in the wardroom and afterwards all the officers came to my cabin. We had some songs, Mr Seymour accompanying on the guitar, and just as the clock struck toasted absent friends and sang "Home sweet home," then to bed. Good night, God bless and keep you.

Jan 1st 1882. – New Year's day. A bright pleasant day to begin the New Year upon. I shall finish this letter here and send it back to Stanley by Mr Cobb to catch the mail of the 18th. – We had Service on the lower deck this morning as it was too cold for the open air, hymns no. 73, 72 and 69 were sung. Mr Cobb has gone on shore just to get some milk and cream for us from his station. Did I tell you that this settlement

Photo: Tony Chater

"The head of a penguin coming out of a hole at the root..." (page 68)

The Jackass penguin (*Spheniscus magellanicus*) nests throughout the Islands in burrows, frequently taking advantage, as here, of the shelter of tussac roots to establish its home. Apart from their burrowing, the most notable characteristic of these birds is a loud, braying call, from which their familiar name derives.

"Loggerhead ducks, a most peculiar species..." (page 68)

Photo: Jane Cameron

The Logger Duck, otherwise known as the Flightless Steamer Duck (*Tachyeres brachypterus*), is endemic to the Falklands, and congregates in small flocks preferring rocky beaches around sheltered harbours and inlets. Breeding pairs become extremely aggressive towards each other. The name "Steamer Duck" apparently derives from the bird's manner of propelling itself through the water, wings flailing, in a way reminiscent of a paddle steamer.

70

consists entirely of the employees of the Falkland Islands Company? There are about fifty persons including a Presbyterian Minister[27] and a doctor, fancy they are all Scotch. Moreover all the shepherds in Lafonia have come in for their new year's holiday, you know what that means from Aberdeen experience. All these thirsty souls have congregated expecting to find a supply of whisky for their jollification. This whisky was sent off from Stanley in a schooner the day we sailed, but hélas, owing to head winds she has not yet arrived and is not likely to for some time as far as I can see; the wind hangs in the S.W. and there is every prospect of its doing so for some little time. You may well imagine the blank looks of these good people and how painfully sober they are as there is not a drop of liquor in the place. There are to be horse races tomorrow amongst them but I fear they will be very *spiritless* affairs.

Still the same Highland look about the country. This harbour is a splendid one, perfectly landlocked, and so far up the Sound that no sea is felt. There are two large wooden houses on shore, one occupied by the minister and the other by the doctor who are both married. Then there is a small barracks for the single men and cottages for the families. On the opposite side of the creek is a large wool-shed, and some half mile away a place for boiling down the sheep for tallow – but I will tell you more about the place after landing tomorrow. I am to interview the overseers to hear whether they can give me any information about the Yankee sealers as the former live on the coast near the seal rookeries.

Jan 2nd. – I have just returned from Darwin. We landed at ten this forenoon, Mr Cobb, the Doctor, Mr Luscombe and self. On the landing we found everyone astir and starting for the race course which is about two miles off in the downs. We were accommodated with steeds, little wiry fellows about fourteen hands with Mexican saddles and headgear. Their pace is an amble, very comfortable when you get used to it but rather trying at first when you fancy the beast is always just going to work himself up to a trot which never comes off. We passed dozens of people, men and women on the way to the course, all riding and

---

[27] The large numbers of Scottish workers employed by the Falkland Islands Company were in need of a minister, and in 1872 the Rev A. Yeoman arrived to take up the post. In the following year a church was erected. This building was moved to Goose Green when the main settlement was transferred in the early years of this century, and now serves as the Community Centre.

"Fancy, they are all Scotch..." (page 71)

Photo: Falkland Islands Museum Collection

The plaid caps and trews of these shepherds indicate their origins. Governor Moody, in a despatch of 1842, was the first to suggest that "the settlers best adapted to colonise these islands would be from among the industrious population of the Orkney and Shetland Islands, accustomed to a hardy life." As wool production expanded during the years that followed, shepherds were routinely recruited from Scotland, prized for their experience in crofting and hill farming. One such was William Blain, working as a shepherd at the time of Wiseman's visit, who later wrote "the Falkland Islands is known as an English colony. But I think that Scotland has equally as good a claim to the Falklands as England. At the time I am speaking of, the majority of the inhabitants was Scotch, or of Scotch descendants." To this day, most Islanders have some Scottish ancestry.

looking very picturesque, the men with their slouch hats and long flowing ponchos lined with red, high boots and long spurs, and the women with gay plaid shawls and skirts. I should imagine there were at least a hundred and sixty horses on the ground, they looked quite like a cavalry regiment bivouacked. I need not describe the personal appearance of either men or women when I tell you they were all Scotch and they looked as if they had been taken off the corner of Market and Union Streets Aberdeen and set down here, all the men smoking and lounging about with their hands in their pockets and talking broad Scotch.

The course was a straight one a thousand yards long. The men all ride bare-backed and go as hard as they can. There were eight races, the first a thousand yards for a silver cup given by Mr Cobb. This was a good race and the horses, three in number, all came in close together. Then followed some short races of four and six hundred yards for small sums of money, then they had a most exciting race in which there were about fifteen entries for a case of whisky which had just been discovered in the settlement. This was ridden furiously and won by a lad of seventeen who will no doubt have many friends this evening.

We got up a race for the blue-jackets who had all landed. This was great fun. They had to ride bare-backed for six hundred yards. About fourteen started but only three arrived, the rest galloping wildly over the country vainly endeavouring to steer their horses, forgetting that you never use the bit with these animals except to stop them but just press the rein against their necks to turn them. Well, off these good people went helter-skelter, some falling off and wildly running after their steeds under the impression they would catch them. They very soon cleared the course of everyone, as they came charging about in all directions at full gallop never attempting to pull up. One man got rather a nasty fall and sprained his arm, he had pulled suddenly at the bridle whilst the horse was full gallop, stopping him dead and shooting over his head as if flung from a catapult.

Lieutenant Luscombe's version of this occasion is as follows:

"We rode out to the annual race meeting, where we found about 200 mounted shepherds who rode some capital races, bareback; after these races we got up a bluejackets' race which was the sport of the day; the great difficulty was to start the 16 who competed; at length we got about 6 off on

Photo: John Leonard

"Then they had a most exciting race..." (page 73)

Horse racing is as popular in the Islands now as it was in Wiseman's day. At the annual Stanley sports meeting, held after Christmas, visitors, especially naval or military, have always been accommodated if they wished to ride. The most notable visitor to participate was the Duke of Edinburgh, who won the Sailor's Race on a local horse in 1957.

the course, and 2 came in the right way; the others were taken charge of by their horses and rode bang into the crowd causing some confusion."

After this we returned to the settlement where Mrs Smith the overseer's wife supplied us with a substantial lunch of the most splendid roast mutton, then an apple tart and oh! such cream. The mother-in-law of this good lady was in Halifax when my grandfather was there as senior officer in 1823; is not that curious? I did not see the old lady as she was out for which I was sorry.

The settlement consists of a manse, a doctor's house, a large barracks for the single men and some ten cottages for the overseer and married men, all built of wood around a green close to the water's edge. I met the minister, a Mr Yeoman, quite a typical Scotch parson. I went to his house to leave my overcoat, and had not been ten minutes there before he informed me of his whole history. Born in Dumfriesshire he came out here as soon as he was called ten years ago, went home after five years and whilst staying with a brother parson met his wife "who was fra' Aberdeen and just keeping house for her brother, and that's how we became acquainted, and I just married and brought her out here to keep house for me, and have been much the more comfortable since, will ye no take a wee drap o' whisky." I declined his offer with thanks and departed.

We start tomorrow once more on our rounds and I must leave this letter with Mr Cobb to take back to Stanley for the mail. May God bless you and keep you, dear wife; you will, I hope, see Capn. Bainbridge in a day or two and get the latest news of *Dwarf* and myself.

Kiss the children and give my love to mother, and now goodbye for the present with all love from your

Ever loving husband.

Jan 3rd. – 7 a.m. Dear wife, just another line to say goodbye. Mr Cobb lands in about half an hour and we start once more on "The Hunting of the Snark." We did not see anything of the cattle corrals yesterday as all the men were amusing themselves and no work doing. But Capn. Packe has promised to take me out and show me some of that work on our return to Stanley.

Please give the compliments of the season to our neighbours in Essex. Tell Mrs Lowndes if she would promise to take a seal around instead of

"All built of wood around a green close to the water's edge..." (page 75)

Photo: Collection of Mrs Eileen Jaffray

Darwin was the headquarters of the Falkland Islands Company's farming operations in Lafonia from the late 1850s until earlier this century, when it was decided to move most of the buildings to Goose Green, a short distance away, but with better access for shipping. The flagstaff atop the hill on the left still stands, and was constructed from the spars of two famous vessels, the *Great Britain*, dismasted while rounding the Horn in 1886, and the Keppel Mission Schooner *Allen Gardiner*. Note the peat smoke drifting above the rooftops, still a characteristic sight in the Islands on a calm day.

her pugs I will try to get her a young one... on second thoughts perhaps she would not see the joke. I hope Lady Ibbetson is quite well and Sir Henry as active as ever with the hounds.

Choiseul Sound
Falkland Islands
Jan 3rd 1882

My darling wife,

After my last letter I bade goodbye to Mr Cobb, and we steamed out of Darwin Harbour, laden with cream, milk and other good things including a lamb which friend Cobb had sent me. It is a fine day and the sea is smooth so on we steam merrily, down the Sound. The 1st Lieut is doing some sketches of our shooting party which I shall send you together with a short account of my own, and you must hand them over to Mr Watson for production in "The Sporting and Dramatic", but make him send you back the sketches[28].

We pass Lively Sound and at its eastern end stop at Motley Island as there is a rookery of hair seals (sea lions), and it is so smooth that I shall pull through the half mile of light kelp and land to see them.

Such a sight, the Doctor and Charlie (our sealer) accompanied me as we neared the point in which the rookery is situated. The great lions raised themselves up on their fore flippers and roared, quite like a shore lion roars. After some difficulty on account of the thick kelp we effected a landing on a small ledge of rock which jutted out into deep water, and scrambled to the beach about fifty yards from the lions. The males are great big fellows about fifteen feet long and some more, with dark brown coats and a mane all round their head and neck. The females are smaller and of a yellow colour; their fur is of no use, only the leather is used for harness. But all the time we were walking up to the "gentle-men," there were about a dozen great lions all roaring and sitting up in a most threatening manner, with their wives and little ones (for every female that we see has one and most of them two pups, little fellows about three or four feet long.)

In we walk, and when about ten yards off the males seem to make a

---

[28] Mr Watson was editor of "The Illustrated Sporting and Dramatic News", a fort-
nightly magazine to which Wiseman was an occasional contributor. Unfortunately
nothing came of this idea to produce an article on the Falklands.

"Roaring and sitting up in a most threatening manner..." (page 77)

The Southern Sea-Lion (*Otaria flavescens*) is the most common of the pinnipeds which frequent the shores of the Falklands. Generally speaking they are not alarmed by the approach of man, nor are they aggressive unless attacked or harassed during the breeding season. However, the domestic life of the male is marked by frequent contests with other males in defence of his territory, harem, and pups.

Photo: Tony Chater

This drawing from *The Illustrated London News* of 1856 is entitled "Falkland Islands – encounter of a sealer with a sea-lion in a tussac bog." It shows the Victorian appetite for melodrama, and also illustrates the hazards of drawing unknown beasts from verbal descriptions only.

79

rush at us. Charlie, whose sealing instincts make him terribly excited, shouts that we should throw stones at them (the beach is all large pebbles) and opens the bowling with an enormous one which catches the nearest lion right in the mouth, he crunches it like cracking a nut in his rage but will not retreat. We fire another volley all taking effect on his head but he only roars the louder and comes towards us. It is all I can do by shouting to keep Charlie back. He has taken his coat off and cut a huge stem of kelp as thick as his arm, this is for a club. The lion advances with a roar, we give him at the same time another volley well directed against his head, I hear a shout on my right and see the gentle Charlie rushing in, luckily for him the lion was turned by the last volley and is in full retreat.

Mrs Lion who has her family to look after has not been so sharp and holds her ground until stunned by a blow from Charlie's kelp club; poor thing, I was afraid he had killed her, she lay so still and the two little pups came flopping along to crawl in beside their mother thinking she was asleep, and bleating just like lambs. There she lies, eight feet of yellow sea lioness, but in a few minutes I am happy to say she shows signs of life. In the meantime all the lions appear head and shoulders out of water close round the point, roaring and making an awful noise.

After inspecting the invalid who begins to get unpleasantly lively and snaps and charges about as she recovers, we retreat about ten yards when up come all the lions again and after a few reassuring roars the ladies and pups follow into the water – it is a most wonderful sight.

To realise what these beasts are like imagine the seal at the zoo grown to about fifteen feet in length and broad in proportion, his head covered with a short thick mane and his mouth armed with as good a set of teeth as his friend the lion a few cages off. If you then imagine behind you long tufts of tussac grass, a boulder beach thickly strewn with kelp, patches of which cover the sea for half a mile around, and about twenty of these enlarged seals lying about the beach, you may then fancy yourself at the Motley Island rookery.

On return to our boat we came across a youngster evidently deserted by its parents. This was too tempting and we took him aboard after a great deal of snapping and bleating, so here he is and the men are feeding the baby on milk through an india rubber tube. It is literally a baby, for Charlie says it cannot be more than fortnight old.

Up went the boat again and on we steamed, anchoring under Bleaker Island for the night, and I went early to bed after a most interesting afternoon.

Rockhopper Penguins

Photo: The Falkland Islands Company

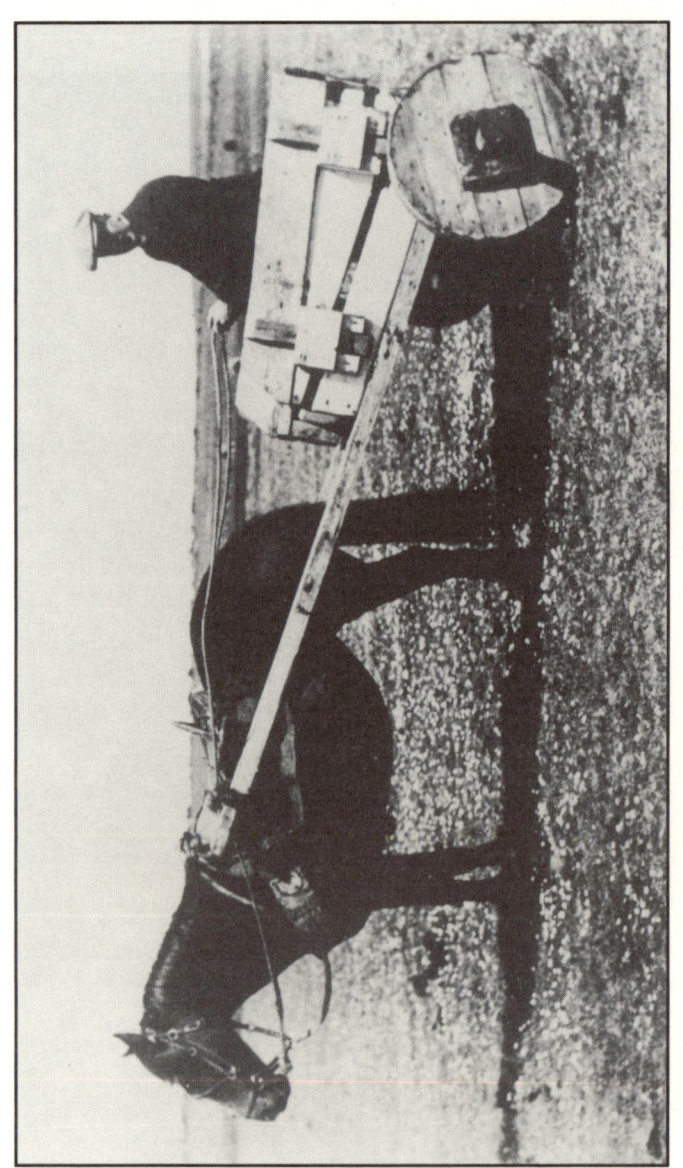

Driftwood cart on Bleaker Island

Photo: Falkland Islands Company; Cobb Collection

Farmers all over the world tend to be versatile people and to make use of whatever materials come to hand, but in the remoter parts of the Falklands this quality seems almost to be raised to an art form.

82

CHAPTER 5

BLEAKER ISLAND, GEORGE ISLAND, BIRD ISLAND

Jan 4th. – I landed this morning taking Luscombe, Horwill and the Doctor with me to see what was to be shot, as there were two ponds marked on the chart about half a mile inland. Twelve couple of snipe were shot on the way up to the ponds, and these latter were covered with wild fowl, duck, teal and widgeon. They could hardly be persuaded to rise, but kept in the centre of the large pond out of shot. By patiently hiding in the tussac while some of the party walked round to the opposite shore we managed to get ten couple of teal, some widgeon and a goose. We returned to the ship after a two hour walk and started for Owen Roads, if possible to look at Driftwood Point where another seal rookery is situated.

Jan 5th. – Darling, by this time you will have got my first letter from *Dwarf* and I hope you will see Capn. Bainbridge and learn all about the private code, and also about the ship. I think you will like the gallant Captain.

Yesterday a N.W. wind came on and rendered it impossible to land at Driftwood Point, but I steamed in as close as the kelp would let me and saw a good many lions on the point who all stood up and sniffed at the ship. On we went, but at one time the weather got so thick and the squalls so heavy that I feared we should not reach our destination, especially as there is a long reef just off the entrance to the roads which one wants clear weather to see. However just as we were getting into Eagle Passage the weather cleared and we ran in, anchoring under George Island at eight o'clock last night.

This morning a shooting party started, Seymour, Luscombe, Doctor and self, accompanied by Charlie who was to show us the wild pigs said to abound in this island. Minto came and one of the boat's crew, also Fennoran the chief gunner's mate whom I allowed to come with a ship's rifle in case any pigs were spotted too far off for the guns. This island is

83

not inhabited and throughout the day we found the greatest difficulty in persuading the birds to get up and be shot at. Off we started for the west side of the island where pigs were said to be, and very heavy work it was tramping over the uneven ground, for between the tufts of grass you went down knee deep.

We walked or rather stumbled on for about three hours. The only incident beyond the tumbles was a sharp attack on my coxswain by two infuriated sea-hens[29] near whose nest he happened to be walking. This was very amusing, the birds (large brown ones about half as big again as Jim) wheeled round his head screaming and finding that would not stop him or drive him from the forbidden ground they soared into the air, then came swooping down right at his head. He had to duck and move his rifle about to keep clear of them, but as soon as he had passed the spot where the nest was they ceased and left him alone. It really would have been rather serious if they had struck him.

On we went for the tussac and arriving at the edge spread across and commenced our pig stalking. The tussac here is quite seven feet high and as we had been told wonderful stories of how the infuriated boars rush at you from their hiding places, you may be sure we kept a sharp look out. I heard a good deal of firing on the right of the line but I saw nothing myself, not even my next neighbour. After about two hours' scramble varied by an occasional fall into a penguin's burrow, I got on top of a sandhill and joined the faithful Minto in a prolonged shout in hopes of attracting the others by sound as we could not see them. This was useless so on we went.

I bore down to the right and shortly found myself by the sea and attracted by a great noise of birds I walked to the edge of a low cliff and found myself all of a sudden in the midst of a shag rookery. The birds were perched on a long ledge of rock overhung by the tussac, the females on their nests out of which popped the heads of their young progeny. It was a most curious sight; there were hundreds of these birds and at least two hundred nests with four or five young ones. The

---

[29] Almost certainly the Falkland Skua (*Catharacta skua antarctica*) which becomes extremely aggressive during the breeding season, and will readily attack any intruder who ventures near the nesting site. Their aerobatics are impressive, and they are skilful at "playing chicken" with humans and dogs, but they have been known to inflict injury by colliding with the objects of their fury.

creatures were so tame that they allowed me to come quite close to them and would not leave the ledge until pushed, when they would make a short circuit and return. I had quite a fight with one old lady who utterly refused to leave the nest until pushed off inch by inch with the aid of my gun barrel. Then finding herself driven off she wheeled round and round in short flights, coming unpleasantly near my face with her long sharp bill until I was obliged to beat a retreat, when she resumed her nest in triumph.

Just after leaving this interesting colony I fell in with some of our party, called a halt, and soon collected our forces for lunch which we were all ready to discuss, except the irrepressible Charlie who would go on a little farther to prospect. He returned in about ten minutes announcing the discovery of a pond close by where he thought there were pigs. I had had so many false alarms that my confidence in Charlie was a bit shaken, so I let Seymour and the gunner's mate go and the rest of us stuck to our lunch. In about five minutes we heard the report of a rifle and then bang-bang, in quick succession from a gun, so leaving Minto to bring on the lunch things off we started, and on getting over the brow of the next hill found not only a pond but a dead pig lying on the opposite side shot by the gunner's mate. It was a fine beast but unfortunately a sow, however I had her head cut off and intend trying to cure it.

The pond was covered with teal and geese, so we lined it round and had a regular battue, the birds flying from one end to the other. We succeeded in getting all the teal off it, the geese we spared as they are so heavy to carry. After collecting our game and taking piggy's hindquarters off we started for another pond in hopes of picking up another pig on the way. The latter hope was doomed to disappointment but again the lake afforded much sport – any number of teal and as luck would have it two silver geese, both of which were bagged and their skins are now being cured for a friend of mine, a lady, can you guess who that lady is?

After this we struck out for the ship. Some of the party captured a lot of wild goslings to add to our bag. On our arrival abreast the ship we shot some geese for the men and embarking in the galley arrived safely on board after a pleasant day. I just had time to change, then got the ship under way and we started for Bird Island and Port Stephens.

We went through a narrow channel between Barren and George Islands which I had sent the Navigating Lieutenant to sound in the morning. The channel was rather narrow and the tide strong; nothing to fear however, except that just as we got into the narrowest and most difficult part, a lot of kelp got round one of the propellers and for some moments we stopped dead. I confess my heart was in my mouth until I just saw her move again, as the tide was setting us right onto the reefs and little could have been done. Had I anchored she would have swung astern into the kelp and fouled *both* screws, when we should have been helpless and certain to have gone on shore, and if a strong breeze had sprung up... However all's well that ends well and on we went, so shaping course for the night we have fifty miles to run and I am off to bed.

Jan 6th. – At 5.30 this morning we stopped opposite Bird Island. It has the appearance of the top of a mountain sticking out of the water so steep are its cliffs. On all sides but one it is covered with tussac to the edge of the cliffs. On the north side is a little bay where the hills slope down to the water's edge; this is the landing place. From the ship we saw innumerable birds flying about, and the whole of one side of the steep hill which joins the east side of the little bay covered with white dots and a great noise constantly coming from this direction.

Off I started in my boat accompanied by the Doctor, Charlie and Minto the faithful. On nearing the shore we were nearly deafened by a noise resembling the combined efforts of all the lambs and hens in the Falklands attempting to drown out each other. This babel proceeded from the penguin rookery where were also a large gull (called Mollimauk[30] by the people here) who had also established a nursery on the side of the hill. The penguins here were most absurd. This sort, the Rock Penguins[31], are the smallest on the island, being about the size of a raven. They have black bodies with a white breast and a yellow crest over each eye. These birds are still more ridiculous than the other sorts as instead of walking they hop along, putting one in mind of a discontented sugar broker. How they get up and down the sides of this steep hill is a wonder, for so steep is it that we had a regular scramble to get even a

---

[30] This is the beautiful Black-Browed Albatross. See page 129.
[31] Normally known as Rockhoppers (*Eudyptes chrysocome*), these are the most common Falkland Islands penguin, although their numbers have declined in recent years. The familiar name aptly describes their habit of making a home on steep, rocky slopes, which they scale with amazing agility.

Photo: *Falkland Islands Museum; Schulz Collection*

"So steep is it that we had a regular scramble..." (page 86)

Rockhopper penguin rookery, West Falkland. A typical nesting-site for this species.

87

short way up to see these birds right up on the crest of the hill two hundred feet high.

We landed on the rocks and stood looking at them. A whole regiment would come out of the water two or three hundred strong, form upon a rock close to the water's edge, and then when apparently all were present start off hopping up the hillside to relieve guard at their different nests. Both birds can never leave the nest and fish together as numbers of kites are hovering about ready to seize on the contents of every unprotected nest. Presently even more noise is heard as the fond couples meet at their nests and relate their adventures, then down come the late sentries, form up in companies on the rock and dive off row after row to fish.

We found evidence of our sealing friends having been on the islands, and from the look of the charred remains of their fire, and some fresh seal blubber lying about, they had only just left. There were two huts built of tussac peat and thatched with grass, no end of egg shells (the Mollimauk's) a cask of beef quite good, and some bullock's horns together with two or three seal clubs – but the birds had flown. We followed a sort of path they had made through the tussac to the seal rookery and after a good half hour's struggle through charred roots (for the island had been set fire to some time ago) we got to the edge of a cliff about twenty feet high under which was a flat ledge of rock on a level with the water. This was the rookery, but no seals were seen although ones olfactory nerves told of the recent presence of those animals. We had our walk for nothing, and still more disgusting was it to have just missed the Yank.

We returned to the ship and started for Port Stephens, as I felt sure some news of these people would be gathered from the settlement there. Just as we turned the headland outside the port what should be seen in a snug little out-of-the-way bay but a schooner, and to my delight in about five minutes up went the American colours. This must be our friend, so we ranged up to him, anchored, and I sent Mr Luscombe to ask the Captain to come on board as I wished to see him.

Luscombe writes:
"On the way up we observed a sealing schooner in Ten Shilling Bay, so

we bore down on her, and anchored close alongside her: I was sent aboard, and brought the captain back: a thoroughgoing Yankee: his schooner was called the Adelia Chase, *35 men mostly Portuguese, a very dirty looking mob: they feed on the seal blubber principally and don't get any pay."*

According to Falkland Islands shipping records, the schooner captain was named Church. The ship had already been around the Islands for over a year on this voyage, and in November of 1881 Governor Kerr had written to the Colonial Office especially mentioning Adelia Chase *as one of the ships causing such depredations to the seal colonies that the introduction of a Close Season had become an urgent necessity.*

In about ten minutes the captain arrived and was ushered into my cabin. What a character! his face the typical stage Yankee, with chin beard and short light hair, a regular Salem Scudder look. His dress was in keeping, a pair of trousers so greasy you could only guess at what the original material was, a brown coat almost in the same condition, canvas slippers, and a muffler round a very dirty neck completed his costume. The coat I should tell you was patched with every conceivable material and quite a Joseph's coat in the matter of colour. Add to this a strong smell of stale seal's blubber and you may imagine what my visitor was like.

He appeared very ill at ease and commenced a long string of explanations as to how he had obtained lease from Mr Hunziker[32] for landing men on Bird Island, and that whilst sealing at Staten Island he heard that an Ordinance was passed prohibiting sealing during the pupping season; that hearing this he, despite the loss entailed by leaving that rookery, immediately started from Staten to take his men away and had done so the day before I arrived; that moreover they only got seven skins during their stay there which had been of two months' duration. After allowing him to finish what he had to say I informed him that I had nothing

[32]John Frederick Hunziker was a Swiss national who had for many years worked in Patagonia with the South American Missionary Society, successfully gaining the confidence of the Teheulche Indians. He subsequently managed Port Stephens farm for J.M. Dean and Sons, and married (sequentially) two Felton sisters. He died in 1907 in the United States and is commemorated at Port Stephens by the name Hunziker's Leap, a chasm 500 feet deep which was cleared by Hunziker on horseback one day while he was chasing colts.

89

whatever to do with what had gone before, but I was here simply to warn him that an Act had been passed the 29th of December last making it illegal to kill seals between October and April, and that I trusted he would not break the law or most assuredly he would be fined £300.

He said of course he would be the last man to break the law, but still he seemed fidgety about something and began a long story of how some masters of sealers were so cruel as to land boats' crews in rookeries where a gale of wind would wash them away, in fact that many sealers were drowned in this way last season, but he could never do this and so lost many skins and was the victim of his own tender-heartedness. (I am told my philanthropic friend was one of the worst offenders in this matter.) Last time he was in Stanley, he said, some of his crew tried to run away but he put them in irons and asked his Consul what he should do, as to wait and prosecute them would be great loss to him, my time (as he put it) is I guess worth £100 a day. "Wall the Consul advised me just to go to sea and say no more about it, so I went aboard that evening determined to sail at daylight. Wall just before turning in I went to see the men in irons and the poor brutes was that cold that I called the First Mate and said, see here you just knock the irons off them cusses and let 'em go and turn in, whilst the mates keep night watch to prevent them running. Wall, just as they were relieving the first watch three of the cusses jumped overboard and swum ashore, I would not wait and sailed at daylight. Wall I hear since that one of them was found drowned in the kelp and that the Governor wanted me for that job, but what had I to do with it if the cuss will jump overboard and drown, I can't be answerable. Wall, I just thought that you Captain had been sent after me for that affair, not that I am afraid for I done nothing."

I am bound to say his looks betrayed him, I never saw anyone so relieved when I told him I knew nothing of this business and only wanted him to understand that he must not come sealing in the Falkland Islands during the close season.

I have heard since that the body was picked up a week afterwards in Stanley Harbour sadly disfigured and so much eaten by birds that it was impossible to prove foul play. The two survivors stated they were swimming ahead of their companion, and that a whale boat was lowered from the schooner and gave chase but they could not say for certain whether the boat overtook the third man or no, but that before they got safely to land she returned to the ship. Of course the proper course, and in fact the only course a decent man could have taken, would have been to report the desertions the following morning instead of shirking off to sea, so the conclusion was naturally arrived at that the skipper or some of his mates had clubbed the man and left as soon as possible.

But to return to our Yankee's visit. He informed me he had been out twenty months, had already sent home 100 fur skins, that he had 480 on board and hoped to make up 600 before the end of season. The price he got for the skins was generally about £5 a piece, principally taken from Staten Island and the coasts of Tierra del Fuego. He told me some of the rookeries were in terribly exposed places, repeating his assurance that he would never do such a thing as expose his men. I then wished him good morning and sent him back to his ship.

This same mild gentleman I since hear was the hero of the following anecdote. It appears these sailing schooners fit out in the State of Maine and sail with just the Captain and four or five mates to the Cape Verde Islands; there they ship about thirty of those poor wretched islanders and away they go for twenty months sealing. The custom is to pay all at the end of the voyage, so the poor crew get nothing but a dollar or two occasionally during the voyage. Well, just as our humane friend had filled up with seal skins and oil he touched at Sandy Point[33] and was so generous as to give all his Cape Verde crew leave, with a dollar each to enjoy themselves. Away they went, but next morning what was their consternation when they found our cute Yankee friend had sailed in the night for the States with all their pay in his pocket.

What a villainous thing, said I to the gentleman Mr Hunziker (of whom more anon). "Oh it is quite the usual thing with the sealers. Few if any of the wretched Portuguese from Cape Verde ever see their homes again, but work is so scarce there that there are always others ready to take their place, tempted by the promise of high wages."

Two seasons ago one skipper left a mate and seven Portuguese to winter in South Georgia in order that he might be first to be sealing in the following spring. Fancy these poor wretches, born and bred in a

[33] Now known as Punta Arenas, although the wood which comes from the area is still called Sandy Point timber in the Falklands.

semi-tropical climate, with nothing but the clothes they shipped in and the few odds and ends of canvas and tarpaulin they managed to pick up on board being sent to winter in such a place. Captain Cook who visited the islands in 1775 in the southern summer wrote: "At 9 a.m. we saw an island of ice, as we then thought, at a distance of 13 leagues." And further: "The head of Possession Bay as well as two places on each side was terminated by perpendicular ice cliffs of considerable height, pieces were continually breaking off with loud explosion. The inner parts of this country were not less savage and horrible. The only vegetation we met with was a coarse strong grass growing in tufts, wild burnet and a plant like moss, which sprang from the rocks." This is its description in midsummer so you may picture it in winter. All the Portuguese were frozen to death and the Yankee mate was found in a wretched state with all those corpses lying about the hut. Evidently the sealer's life is not a happy one.

Some of these schooners have been known to take a great number of skins. One skipper got 10,000 in one season and sensibly retired. The average is about four hundred and it takes six hundred to make a successful voyage. They do not kill more than three out of every hundred they see, the animals are so wary, unless they catch them with their young whom the poor beasts will not leave and are consequently all killed whilst the young die of starvation, their skins being no good.

I fear you will be very tired of this long yarn about seals, but as I took rather an interest in getting these few facts together I must inflict them upon you.

After bidding adieu to our American cousin I started on for Port Stephens.

CHAPTER 6

PORT STEPHENS, BEAVER ISLAND, NEW ISLAND

I anchored off the settlement at Port Stephens at noon. It is quite an imposing place, some half dozen houses and a large wool-shed all painted white with red roofs, and looking neat and well kept. The whole character of the West Falklands is quite different from the East. High bold headlands and good ranges of hills are the ruling feature, while the grass looks more luxuriant and homelike. The property all about here belongs to Mr Dean (whom I have already mentioned) and is managed by Mr Hunziker, a Swiss, and seemingly a good fellow. He came off to call at once and offered his services in getting anything possible for us, and placed horses at the disposal of all the officers. I went in the evening to return his call and found him in a very nice wooden house with a good conservatory and well kept garden.

Jan 7th. – A wet morning, so instead of going for a ride with Mr Hunziker I shall do some more writing...

I got so sick of writing all day that I went on shore about five this evening and had a short walk. It was too late for riding. Mr Hunziker very kindly gave me a sea-otter skin.

Jan 8th. – A fine morning but windy. The whole male and female population is coming off to church this morning; I will give you an account later on. I did not tell you that Mr Hunziker quite agrees with me that the farmers if they choose are quite able to protect the seal fisheries, and that they do most thoroughly protect their sheep and cattle from the sealers' raids. In fact the American schooners dare not come after being warned off, and that should they do so he could turn them off any island on his estate and have them at his mercy, as they have to get all their provisions from him.

We were disappointed of the female part of our congregation as the weather looked so threatening, but about fifteen men and children came off including Mr Hunziker and three of his dogs. The Service went off

93

very well, the men singing with a will to make up perhaps for not having turned up for choir practice with Luscombe last night.

Luscombe writes in his journal:
On Sunday all the inhabitants came onboard to church, and our men landed in the afternoon – the pay of an ordinary shepherd here is £5 a month with meat and housing found, so a steady man can save easily: every man is allowed a bottle of rum a week, and nothing more in the shape of drink can be bought anywhere: they are also allowed as much milk as they wish for."

After Service the Hunziker family lunched with me. I landed at four and went for a walk over the hills with Horwill. I will not describe the country again except to say that the hills are much higher, some as much as seven hundred feet. After our walk we went to Mr Hunziker's house and there met the Doctor who had been out after some fern plants, very pretty ones of which he has given me some. I have also been presented with a wild fuschia plant from Tierra del Fuego; it is safely installed in my after cabin and I hope will thrive. The Doctor and Horwill dined with me.

Jan 9th. – Such a catastrophe last night. Just after my guests had bidden me goodnight, I called for my steward to get my bed ready. He answered but did not turn up for some minutes. Then I thought I heard someone fall, and opening my cabin door saw Percival stretched out on the deck. I called the quartermaster to get a light whilst I undid his collar, and soon the Doctor came up and after a little got him to bed. He had had a regular fit, and the Doctor fears it was epilepsy. Percival tells me he has never had one before, but that he went out for a ride yesterday afternoon and felt over tired ever since.

We sailed for Beaver Island at eight this morning where we arrived at three this afternoon. Previously to our departure my friend Mr Hunziker came off to say goodbye, bringing me besides the sea-otter skin a large collection of sea birds' eggs which is very interesting. Off we steamed down the grand harbour of Port Stephens, then passed our old friend Bird Island.

The land all along this part of the coast is very wild and grand, rocky cliffs rising sheer out of the sea, some to as much as seven hundred feet, with the grass all dead and brown and their summits showing the marks of sea and foam during the heavy southerly gales, and most undermined and cut into the strangest shapes by the force of the sea.

We ran through Tea Channel between Tea[34] and Weddell Islands, where there is a terrible tide which simply raced us through at the rate of twenty miles an hour. It was rather nervous work whilst it lasted which I am happy to say was not more than an hour. We are now in a most snug little anchorage, with just room for the ship to swing round. You could not tell by looking around how she got in as we are completely surrounded by hills and seem anchored in the middle of a small mountain loch.

The head shepherd, Mr MacGregor, came off and informed us in broad Scotch that the island belonged to Mr Walcheron[35] who lives at Port Howard in the Western Falkland. This island holds at present about six thousand sheep and MacGregor has four hands besides himself. He is of a very cheerful disposition, enjoyed the life, and told me that until last autumn he had not been off Beaver Island for seven years. Once for five months he was on the island entirely alone, as far as human beings were concerned, but just his doggie. He is just a farmer bodie frae Argyllshire and was a wee laddie minding the sheep on the moors there.

He, as usual, for at every place we stop at it is the same, insisted on sending off three sheep for the ship. We have got such a lot on board now that the upper deck looks more like a stockyard than a man of war's deck. The men are getting so fat and lazy they can hardly move – milk, cream and butter is also sent off in any quantity, this is hospitality! But fancy a country where all the men employed get their meat free, as much as they like of the primest beef and mutton with an unlimited supply of milk, where they feed their pigs off legs of mutton and wild geese, and nobody ever thinks of walking as all he has to do is to catch a horse and saddle him.

Mr MacGregor is going to take us over to where there is a fur seal rookery, but he fears we shall see no seals as they have been a good deal

---

[34]Tea Island was so named by Boston sealers in memory of a certain party.
[35]The name should be *Waldron*. The shepherd was evidently a Gaelic speaker, from whom "Waldron" would to English ears sound rather like "Walcheron". Two weeks later at Port Howard Wiseman was to meet James Waldron, a Wiltshire man, who in 1867 had become the first farmer to take up land on West Falkland.

"The head shepherd, Mr MacGregor...told me he had not been off Beaver Island for seven years..." (page 95)

A remote life for Mr MacGregor, but usually he was not on his own. At the time the nine thousand acres held about six thousand sheep. Today the island is run as a family farm, with just under two thousand sheep.

Photo: Wiseman Collection

"The upper deck looks more like a stockyard..." (page 95)

It is still common for mutton carcasses to be carried for food on the decks of small boats working around the Islands. This photograph was taken in 1990, on the same route that Wiseman travelled between Beaver and New Island. The rocks in the background are known as The Colliers. The boat is the present day *Foam*, once owned by Kitty and Cecil Bertrand of Carcass Island, and now belonging to Tony and Annie Chater of New Island.

Photo: Jane Cameron

frightened lately. However it will be an hour's gallop and we shall get a look at the country. The men are to go in the middle of the day with the net to get a haul of fish which are very plentiful about here. And now good-night and God bless my wife.

Luscombe tells us:

"A seining party left the ship at noon on the 10th and cast the net across the head of the bay, and hauled an immense quantity of fish, about 340 large mullet. The people ashore presented us with as much mutton, milk and penguins' eggs as we wanted."

Jan 10th. – A lovely morning without a breath of wind, and 9 a.m. saw the Doctor, Seymour and myself accompanied by MacGregor start on horseback for Cape Percival under whose cliffs the seal rookery is situated. A glorious ride of about an hour brought us to the edge of the cliff. The day was so clear and bright that all the islands for forty miles round were laid out like a map at our feet, with a smooth sea and not a ripple. Dismounting we crawled to the edge, and looking down five hundred feet below we saw a number of fur seals on the flat ledges of rock just on a level with the water. They looked at first like a lot of enormous leeches crawling up the rocks all shining and wet. Through glasses we saw them very well and counted about forty or fifty together.

How we anathematized the Close Season Act, for with a rifle we could have got at least fifteen or twenty skins, by shooting the beasts as they lay on the rocks and sending a boat round to pick them up. However it was out of the question, so we sat and watched our furry friends playing about and had to leave them in peace. They are not like the seal you see ordinarily, for instead of the round head of the Aquarium Seal they have a long snout with a head just like a large dog.

We rode round the headlands of Beaver Island, and I think I never saw finer rock scenery, so wild and grand the cliffs, four hundred and as much as eight hundred feet rising sheer out of the water. MacGregor was very communicative and pointed out many wild plants, including a sort of strawberry, the leaves a very pretty-coloured green, the fruit looking something like our mountain strawberry but tasting more like the raspberry. He also informed me that the average weight of fleece in these islands was from seven to nine pounds, and that the sheep skin and

Photo: Jane Cameron

"They looked at first like a lot of enormous leeches..." (page 98)

Falkland Fur Seals (*Arctocephalus australis australis*) on West Falkland. Of the four species of pinnipeds breeding in the Falklands, the Fur Seal is perhaps the most apprehensive of man, and their rookeries tend to be in isolated spots with difficult access.

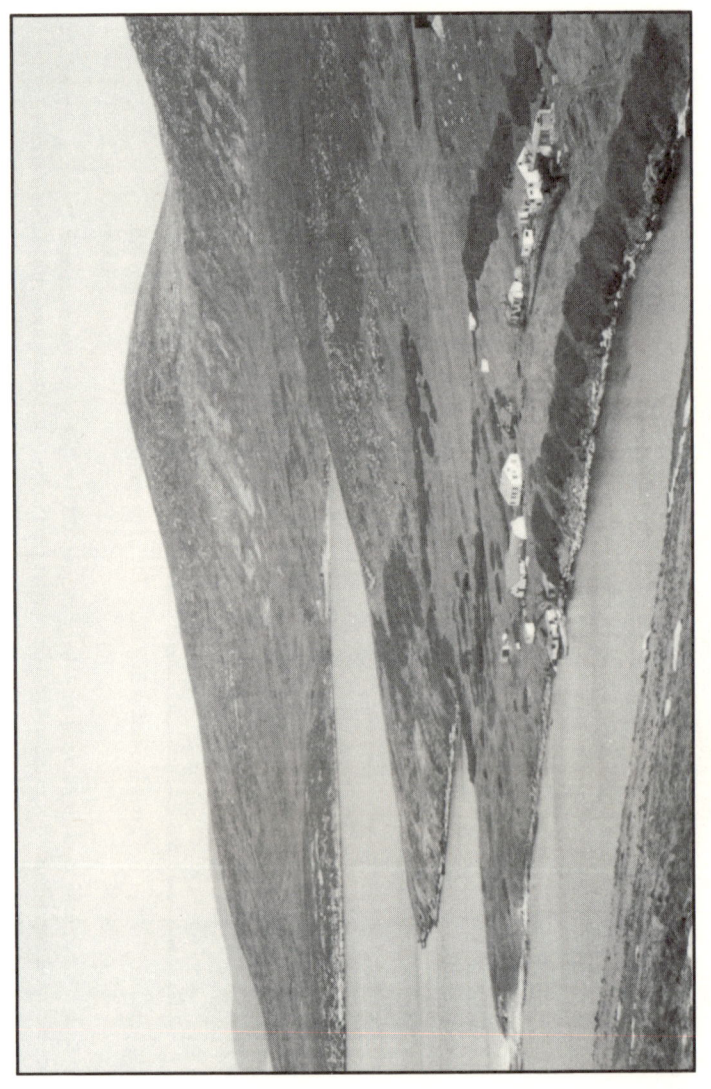

Photo: Jane Cameron

"We steamed across to New Island..." (page 101)

New Island settlement today. The old stone house in which the Dicksons lived is on the right.

fat that is boiled down is worth ten shillings. Mutton seems no object for I had to refuse three sheep offered to the men, they have so much on board.

On our return we lunched with the worthy cicerone[36] and then went down to the head of the creek to await our seining party in the charge of Mr Luscombe. They shot the net across the narrow end of the creek and in one haul got over six hundred fish, what do you think of that? They were grey mullet ranging from twelve pounds to five but principally the larger fish. The gig was laden with them, and as soon as we got on board all hands began splitting them and getting ready to salt them. I was promised a King Penguin[37] but like pie-crust this was broken, so I have to bid adieu to Beaver Island and MacGregor without it.

We steamed across to New Island ten miles off where I found the other sealer I wanted, a wretched little cutter of ten tons called *The Two Sisters* belonging to Stanley. The skipper one Janson came on board and I read him the Act. Poor man he was very down in the mouth about it, having left Stanley in June long before this ordinance and fitted out for a twelvemonth as usual (for which outfit he is in debt for £70). Just as there is a chance of getting something, he is now obliged to desist. I think it is very hard luck – but no doubt he will be able to get a seal or two on the sly.

I landed afterwards and found another Scot looking after the island, Dickson by name. He took me up to his house where we found Mrs Dickson and a family of eight ranging from a baby in arms to a boy of sixteen. Mrs D gave me a delicious cup of milk, and then told me all her troubles. They have been four years on the island, the only bodies there and no doctor to be got at. She has however managed safely to increase the population by two with no ill results, and as the good lady with one baby of four and a half months old had been out all day riding across the rough country helping to drive the sheep in she cannot be a very delicate party. Their great trouble seemed to be their want of mails; they only get them in the shearing season when the schooner comes for wool, so that

[36] One who shows strangers the sights; a guide.
[37] The King Penguin (*Aptenodytes p. patagonica*) is one of the scarcer species of Falkland Island breeding penguins, and the largest. There are scattered rookeries around the Islands, and the colourful presence of a lone King is sometimes detectable among a colony of Gentoos.

it generally takes eighteen months ere they get an answer from home.

They see a good many American whale ships coming in to water and I fancy make a pretty good thing out of them by selling provisions etc. Dickson is a good gardener and cultivates potatoes and cabbages to a large extent.

One peculiarity of the Dickson family is that from constantly mixing with Yankee whalers they have engrafted on their broad Scotch way of talking many Yankee idioms. For instance, when I asked the good lady whether she did not find it lonely sometimes, she said in the broadest Scotch accent, "Ah weel, I canna say but what I do feel lonely sometimes, but I guess we fix up somehow."

This has been a perfect day, bright sun and not a breath of wind. I only hope the day after tomorrow may be as good for our visit to the Jason Islands.

Jan 11th. – Another bright day. Captain Janson paid his respects this morning and asked if I could let him have some provisions, so I got him two or three pieces of pork and some tea and sugar, together with a bag of biscuit. He was so grateful that on his return to the cutter he sent me the skin of a young fur seal perfect, so you shall have a stuffed baby seal from the Falklands if nothing else.

I sent a boat on shore about eleven to bring off Mr and Mrs Dickson, as they had expressed a wish to see the ship. Off they came, he was in his usual costume but Madame was resplendent in a black silk dress and smart hat trimmed with white feathers. She was very ill at ease in her Sunday clothes, in fact from the convulsive way in which she clutched at the skirt I feared that during her tour round the upper deck this article of clothing would have been left behind. They had never been aboard a man-of-war before and were intensely astounded at all they saw, especially the great gun of six and a half tons. This astonished them beyond measure, as did also the engine room. "Eh!" (remarked the lady) "but it's just wonderful what things they invent to kill a body." I got them into my cabin and gave them lunch, after which they landed expressing themselves delighted.

I went on shore some hours afterwards and, mine host having supplied me with a horse and his eldest son coming as guide, off we started. First we rode through a large penguin rookery, and just beyond a rookery of Mollimauk. These latter were so tame that you could almost touch them ere they would move and then they only hopped out of the way a foot or two, their young and the young penguins looking like large balls of grey fluff just able to waddle about.

At our next rookery the inmates were not so friendly; they were the sea hens I have before spoken of. The first intimation I had of our trespass was hearing a whish in the air and finding my hat knocked over my eyes, this was one of the birds swooping at me and who had just missed my head. "Keep your whip going" shouted my companion, "and don't dodge your head down until they are close upon you" – for by this time they were swooping at us from all directions and I had my hat nearly knocked off twice. Just as we got in the thick my companion again repeated his instructions adding "If they do strike you they will stun you and knock you off your horse!" I confess it was very difficult to keep from bobbing your head when you saw a great bird as large as a barndoor fowl coming swooping straight at you and going fifty miles an hour, and I was not sorry when we got clear of their domain and they left us in peace.

On we rode to a high cliff called Landsend. There is a most extraordinary crevasse in the rock here, looking like the perpendicular shaft of a giant mine. The rock rises up sheer all round seven hundred feet, and at one corner you can just get near enough to the edge to see the sea at the bottom of this gigantic well. In rough weather the sea roars and foams through subterranean passages and throws its spray up to the mouth. – It is a most wonderful looking place. If you throw a stone down it crashes and roars with an almost deafening echo. There are three of these strange places in the island, one whose mouth is only a hole six feet across and some hundred yards from the edge of the cliff which is very dangerous and down which many sheep are lost.

On our return I found the lad had a seal skin to sell. It is I fear not a good one, but I gave him six yards of serge for that and as a largesse for having shown me the island. Our baby seal you will be glad to hear is doing well up to date.

Luscombe had this to say about New Island:
"We anchored in a beautiful little harbour. A Scotchman, and family farm the whole of New Island: sheep and cattle. Landed the next day shooting snipe, got one and managed to blow the end of the muzzle off my

gun. Came across some very curious birds called Fire Birds[38] who live underground, only coming out at night. The penguins of which there are millions on the Falklands are most amusing looking birds, looking like parsons with the bands on: they can't get about very well onshore, but waddle about helplessly, and can be driven like sheep."[39]

[38] These beautiful little birds, the Slender-Billed Prions, still live and breed on New Island in large numbers. They may have become known as Firebirds because they seem to be attracted to light, and a fire burning as they return to their burrows at nightfall will reveal large numbers of them in the surrounding area. It is not true that they are entirely nocturnal creatures. During the summer breeding season they feed at sea, far from land, during daylight hours. But in order to protect themselves from predators such as skuas they leave before dawn and return after dusk, so are most in evidence during the hours of darkness.

[39] As a few surviving penguin corrals around the coast testify. At one time penguins were boiled down for their blubber, each penguin giving approximately one pint of oil, the sale of which was an occasional sideline for many a nineteenth-century sealer.

CHAPTER 7

THE JASONS, WEST POINT, CARCASS ISLAND

Jan 12th. – We left New Island at seven last evening, and at four this morning were off the Jason Islands, an account of which I will give you tomorrow. Having been up since three this morning and on my legs all day I do not feel quite up to writing this evening, so I shall say goodnight and God bless my dear wife.

Jan 13th. – It is blowing a gale and as thick as pea soup. Fancy our good luck in having done the Jasons, and being safely anchored in Hope Harbour. And now to tell you of yesterday's doings.

At 5 a.m. we steamed into the channel between Grand and Steeple Jason, disturbing a large herd of hair seals on the little island on the left as we steamed close past them. The lions roared in a most startling manner. A boat was shortly lowered and Horwill, Charlie and myself, accompanied by my henchman Minto, landed on Grand Jason and walked over the south side of the island to where the fur seal rookery was. Charlie was sure of seeing at least two or three hundred. So on we trudged in a great state of excitement, and after a good struggle through the high tussac and a steepish climb over the spur of the hill we arrived at the lip of the rocks under which the rookery is situated, but not a seal or the sign of one was to be seen, much to Charlie's astonishment and chagrin. We roasted him tremendously about his having been so certain that the whole place would be alive with seals, and pressing upon us the necessity of silence when we were at least two miles away from the spot, begging me to allow him to kill just one for a curio, for which amiable purpose he had dragged a heavy sealer's club all the way with him.

It was a lovely morning and notwithstanding our disappointment I enjoyed the walk immensely. The rocks on the hillside were covered with the most magnificent lichens, much finer than those I sent you from Sparrow Cove, and I enclose a specimen. The islands are just the

105

same as the main in appearance, not a tree to be seen and the same Highland look about the hillsides.

Just as we got back on the beach where the boat was, a most amusing incident occurred. A stray hair seal was seen coming out of the tussac and slowly making his way to the water. The faithful Minto got very excited and wanted to try his hand at clubbing the animal, so feeling pretty sure of the result I let him go away. Off he went over the slippery rocks handling his club, but when he got near the seal which was a young one about twelve feet long he slackened his pace. The animal turned round and looked at him, and this was too much for Minto who stopped dead. Then the beast roared and my valiant henchman retreated a little, but we laughed at him so much that he nerved himself for a tremendous blow. Swinging the club over his head he advanced, but just at the critical moment when the club should have come down on the seal's head up went Minto's heels and he was deposited on his back. The animal turning quietly away slid off the rock into deep water. It was lucky for Minto, as had the beast been savage he would certainly have been bitten as he lay quite at the lion's mercy. You may imagine my worthy coxswain has been pretty well roasted by his shipmates about this little incident.

We then got into the boat and pulled across the channel to the little island on which we had seen the sea lions, Horwill wishing to make a closer acquaintance with these gentry. It was just such another scene as at Motley, but the lions were not quite so big nor the cubs so numerous.

We then returned to the ship and went round the north side of Grand Jason. Here, seeing a hut, I sent Mr Luscombe on shore to discover whether anyone was there and if so to warn them against sealing out of season, but on his return he reported the hut deserted, but these wretched people had left two dogs behind them. The poor beasts were hanging around the hut awaiting the return of their masters.

"I went ashore," says Luscombe, "to see if there were any inhabitants, but there was no one there, except two dogs. In the huts were plenty of sheepskins, some paraffin oil, an axe, a hammer, and a cask full of something. I also for the first time saw some large hair seal asleep on the rocks: they are enormous animals weighing as much as one and a half tons: they flop about helplessly, and can be killed easily by a blow on the

forehead: but their skins are not valuable, about 7 shillings being the highest price: the fur seal are the valuable kind and consequently much harder to get at: they must be shot from a distance: their skins fetch as much as £5 in England."

After safely getting through the numerous reefs which surround the Jasons we anchored in Hope Harbour where I shall remain until the blow is over. Fancy our luck in weather, if the blow had come twenty-four hours sooner we should have been close off the Jasons surrounded by reefs and the weather so thick that you could hardly see the ship's length ahead. We should have been in a most unpleasant situation as there is no clear harbour to run for when off these islands.

I fear you will be getting very tired of the Falkland Islands, dear wife, but I can talk of nothing else; no letter from you to answer and I fear I shall not get one until we reach Stanley, so you must excuse these boring descriptions.

Jan 14th. – Yesterday afternoon the wind moderated, and the Doctor came on shore with me to see if there was anything to shoot as the ground looked likely for snipe. We tramped over the country but no sign of a snipe, all we saw was a number of skeletons and carcasses of cattle laying about in all directions. We both came to the conclusion that some awful murrain had visited the cattle in this part of the country, but on enquiry afterwards from two of the overseers of West Point Island we were told that these cattle had all been killed by their owner simply for their hides, the only valuable part of the beasts here. Later on we came across some quite fresh carcasses with plenty of good beef on them just being eaten by the carrion birds. As we found no snipe we returned to the ship just shooting some geese for the men.

It has been blowing hard all the forenoon but there is a bright sky overhead and a warm sun. I am hard at work with all the ship's business, returns of all kinds, gunnery, steam, etc. so shall not I think get on shore. On Monday we start for Carcass Island stopping on the way at West Point to shoot wild cattle, as the owners want the hides and no doubt will give our men the beef.

Luscombe writes:
"At 7 p.m. two brothers Felton came on board from West Point Island

where they have 1,000 sheep and wild cattle, which they are trying to exterminate. From them I learnt the following particulars about sheep farming: an ordinary sheep lasts 3 years for his wool, and gives during that time on an average 25 lbs wool, which varies in price from 1/2d. to 9d a lb: the sheep is then boiled down for tallow, which fetches a good price. The Falkland Island Company own over 100,000 sheep."

Jan 15th. – Another bright sunny day. Our Service went off well, the singing was better than usual as the choir had a practice last evening. I have been misled about this place, having been told there was plenty of shooting and there is none. This afternoon some of the officers and myself are going for a long stretch to a penguin rookery some three or four miles away. We have to get over two steep ranges of hills and then climb up to the top of Death's Head cliff to get to the rookery and this will make what the Yankees would call "quite a difference" – so don't laugh and be cheeky at my three mile long stretch.

10 p.m. "And we did not catch that whale..." No, and you *may* laugh, for after a two hours' climb up one of the steepest hills I have ever tried (1,390 ft. high) when we all thought we were there, on looking round we found between us and the rookery a long valley and steep hill the other side. In fact the place was about ten miles further on, so down we sat and smoked our pipes and voted that penguins looked better at a distance. However we had a good walk and a most enjoyable afternoon and got back to the ship very tired and hungry.

Jan 16th. – A grand day's sport. We left Hope Harbour at half past seven and went to West Point Island where we anchored by eight o'clock. I landed with the Doctor, Horwill, and Luscombe, bringing rifles as well to take the chance of back shots at the cattle. The Feltons met us and had a spare horse for me to ride. Off we started to the other side of the island, and we all posted up the side of the hill behind rocks and high tufts of a sort of moss which grows up to a great height and looks like a large stone covered with close growing moss, this being formed by layers of the dead plant upon which the fresh shoots grow[40]. Away went the Feltons to drive the wild cattle past us.

[40] These would be Balsam Bogs (*Bolax gummifera*) so called because of the resinous fragrance of the gum secreted by the plant. They have been known to grow over three feet high and six feet in diameter.

108

"The Feltons met us..." (page 108)

Arthur Ernest Felton (1854-1933) was the sixth son of Sergeant-Major Henry Felton, late of the Life Guards, who had arrived in the Islands in 1849 with a group of military pensioners selected as colonists for the under-populated settlement. Arthur Felton farmed West Point Island for over fifty years, sometimes assisted by one of his brothers. In 1884 he married Elizabeth (Lillie) Whaits, whose father worked with the South American Mission on Keppel Island. West Point is farmed today by Roddy Napier, great-nephew of Arthur Felton.

Photo: with kind permission of R.B. Napier

109

After waiting about an hour we saw some red and black objects coming down the opposite hill. On they came at a great pace and presently we could make them out as cattle. They came to the bottom of the hill when suddenly the old bull who was leading halted and threw up his head sniffing danger, and after looking round led the herd away to the left and about six hundred yards away from us into a dip which ran up the hillside. Bang went all the rifles below me, and presently I saw just the head of my friend the bull above the rise at a good trot. When opposite me I let fly at two hundred yards. I could not see much of him but noticed he seemed to stop short after the shot, but a second afterwards on he went, and disappeared over the brow of the hill with the rest.

We waited a little to collect our forces and found no damage had been done by the volley. On we went over the hill to some rocky ground where our hosts thought we might get near the beasts if they had turned up the hill after disappearing instead of down to a tussac valley. We mounted and rode on to the crest and saw the herd about a quarter of a mile away sure enough among the rocks. So as soon as the rest of our party arrived we began the stalk. It was heavy work as the boulders of rock were far apart and we had to crawl from one to the other with rifles slung over our backs. After about an hour of this work I saw our friends some three hundred yards away. I gave the signal to try and get a little nearer, but unfortunately our friends sighted something and began moving off, so up we got and gave them a volley. Over rolled a young heifer to Luscombe's rifle whilst a cow fell to the rear looking very sick as the result of the Doctor's shot. My bull meantime detached himself from the rest and made slowly for the tussac bogs away to the left, the wounded cow getting down to the tussac in front of us.

I started off with one of the Feltons in pursuit of my friend the bull, and after a sharp ride of twenty minutes came up with him amongst some bushes, so off I got and went for him. I worked round above him just clear of the bushes trying to get a shot, but he dodged me for a long time and at last I got desperate and walked down towards him. When I got within about fifty yards he turned and shook his head at me as much as to say you had better leave me alone. I got my rifle up and was just going to let fly when he turned short and dived into the brush wood.

110

On I went wishing sincerely he would stand still instead of enticing me into the thick brush wood. However I had not gone ten yards when my friend turned again and showed himself, bellowing and turning up the ground with his head. This I thought should be put a stop to ere he did the same with me, so I took a careful aim and dropped him with a bullet just behind the shoulder. He proved to be a grand old bull with a fine pair of horns which I intend making a trophy of.

My guide thought there were more beasts in the tussac so we went on, and had not ridden for more than a few hundred yards when my companion who was ahead signalled *more cattle*. Off I jumped, and getting up on a tussac bog saw my friends the bulls. I let fly at the nearest of them, a fine white and black fellow and with a lucky shot brought him down, the other a young black bull I fired at but only hit him in the neck and off he went. After taking this gentleman's horns off we went in pursuit of number two, but he would not turn so we headed him and drove him down to the rest of the party when he was polished off in the valley by a shot from Mr Horwill's rifle.

We now thought of getting homewards as our sport had taken us to the far end of the island, so back we started and after a couple of hours of rough walking (for I made Horwill, who is very delicate and easily knocked up, take the horse) we got back to the bay and were rewarded for our exercise by a long drink of the most delicious milk.

One of the Feltons whilst riding home came across some more wild cattle and went for one to lasso him, but whilst going full sprint his girths gave way and we saw him turn a somersault over the horse's head and land on the ground all of a heap. It was a soft falling so up he got again and having repaired damages started in pursuit, and managed to lasso the beast who finding he could make nothing of him by pulling turned and charged, just catching the horse's flank with his horn. Felton then managed to throw him and despatched him with his knife. The horse I am glad to say was not much hurt.

On our arrival on board I sent a party of men to bring in as much beef as they wanted, the hides being all that the Feltons required and had we not taken the meat it would have been left for the birds to eat.

Jan 17th. – This morning at 8 a.m. we bade adieu to West Point

111

Island and its kindly owners, and started for Carcass Island[41] arriving at ten o'clock. It is a lovely day and I hope to get a ride this afternoon. I sent a boat in for Captain Hansen who owns both the island and a fine schooner the *Foam*; she was Lord Dufferin's yacht from which he wrote *Letters from High Latitudes*. Her present owner is the great sealer of these islands and is also one of those who complained about the American sealers shooting his sheep on Grand Jason. He arrived on board in due time and I read him the Ordinance. He is a Dane by birth and seems a very nice fellow.

Hurrah, hurrah!... I am able to get a dozen seal skins from Hansen for a lady I know, he tells me five of them will make a cloak reaching down to the knee[42]. Of course these skins are just as they were taken off the animal's backs, only salted to preserve them, so when they get home they will have to be sent to a furrier for plucking and tanning and then to some trustworthy place to be made up. Perhaps the manager at Howell and Jones, Mr Whatsisname who showed us over, would be able to tell you of a good furrier and afterwards get them made up. With twelve you will be able to make yourself a suit. I am delighted as I was getting very much afraid that I should leave the Falklands without getting my skins. These were taken off the Grand Jason, the very rookery we went to and saw over.

In the afternoon I landed and went for a ride round the island with Mr Hansen. He seems a very decent sort of man, and told me his history which is remarkable. He arrived in Stanley just twenty years ago, in a long boat of a German ship which he, with the rest of the crew, had to abandon in a sinking condition off the Falklands; he at that time was a man before the mast. Sealing was then in full swing, in fact almost the only industry of the colony. So our friend shipped in a sealing cutter of ten tons, the hands all having a share in the take. After a successful cruise or two he saved enough money to buy a share in the vessel which of course gave him a larger number of shares in the sealing, and so on until he was able to buy the cutter up entirely and start for himself. Then he helped to shift sheep from the different islands out of sealing time and

---

[41] Named after H.M.S. *Carcass* which arrived in the Falklands in 1766 to help establish the settlement at Port Egmont. In February of that year she sounded the harbour and surveyed around the lovely island that now bears her name.

[42] According to Luscombe, his captain paid £2 each for these skins.

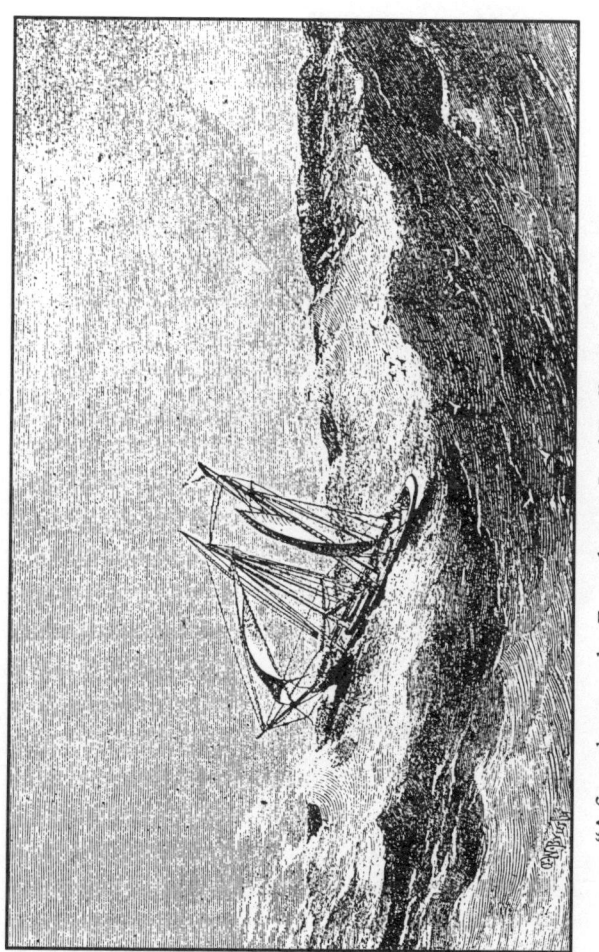

"A fine schooner, the *Foam*, she was Lord Dufferin's yacht…" (page 112)

Illustration: with permission from the Merlin Press

An eighty-eight ton yacht, framed in oak, the *Foam* was built for Lord Dufferin in Portsmouth in 1848 and registered in Waterford. In 1863 she was purchased for £900 by the Falkland Islands Company for use as a mail schooner, and served in this capacity until 1872 when she was bought by Andreas Pitaluga. Ownership subsequently passed to Charles Hansen of Carcass Island, who sailed her for ten years until she was wrecked on Carcass Reef in 1890. The drawing above is one of the illustrations from Lord Dufferin's book "Letters from High Latitudes." The original figurehead of the *Foam* is now in the museum in Stanley.

"He is a Dane by birth and seems a very nice fellow..." (page 112)

Captain Charles Hansen had arrived in the Falklands in 1860 when his ship, the *Concordia*, had foundered after rounding Cape Horn. Some ten years later he acquired the leases of Carcass Island and the Jasons, and began sheep-farming, but continued a sea-faring life, running passengers and freight around the Islands and over to the mainland, and becoming a valued source of information to the government on shipping and shipwrecks. He was also involved in sealing on the Jasons, and concerned about the depredations of poachers, so would have particularly welcomed the *Dwarf* in her capacity as a patrol ship. Captain Hansen was lost at sea on a voyage from Patagonia in 1891. His family continued to farm Carcass Island until 1953.

Photo: with kind permission of Mrs Sydney Miller

114

was enabled to buy a larger vessel, a small schooner. Then he brought the *Foam* out from England, and took voyages over to the Patagonian coast and down to the Straits of Magellan sealing. Then he got married to a maid[43] of the governor's wife, Mrs Robinson. He speaks so nicely of his wife and children who are now in England and how well she managed for him, and how much of his success he owes to her – dear wife, how much I thought of you. Well, after these ventures he rented the islands he now has, gradually stocking them with sheep until he now has some three thousand of them, still keeping his schooners going and sailing one himself.

He took me round his island to show me all his sheep and was very proud of them. It is a good island and the grass upon it rich. The cream he sent me was just as thick as any Devonshire cream you ever saw. In the evening he dined with me and brought off a most lovely sealskin waistcoat to show me the sort of fur on my skins, and told me his was of exactly the same sort. I do hope they will make my wife some handsome furs. I shall most likely send them off by steamer for Monte Video in a cask. I shall also put in the skin of the seal pup which should not be sent to the furriers but to someone to stuff as he is, without being plucked, and then you will see what the beasts are like when taken. Mind the skins will look very dirty and probably smell not a little when they arrive but that is nothing, all seal skins are sent home in the same way, and a good furrier will soon put them right, and can be trusted to give you back your own skins. They are my New Year's gift to my dear wife.

[43]This was Julia Sarah Spittle. They married in Stanley on 18 March 1869. They had five children, and their son Jason continued to farm Carcass until his death in 1952.

115

"A few of the ruined walls are still standing…" (page 117)

The remains of the first British settlement at Port Egmont on Saunders Island.

The site was originally surveyed, and named, by Commodore John Byron ("Foul-weather Jack") in 1765 who said of the harbour "the whole navy of England might ride here in perfect security from all winds." The settlement was established by Captain John MacBride in 1766 and maintained as a naval base. A ship was built here in 1773 out of imported timber, and commissioned as H.M.S. *Penguin*. In the following year the base was abandoned as part of the defence cuts, or as Lord Rochford put it, "as a small part of an economical naval regulation."

The site was never again inhabited, and presents much the same picture today as it did at the time of Wiseman's visit.

Photo: Jane Cameron

CHAPTER 8

KEPPEL ISLAND, PEBBLE ISLAND, PORT HOWARD

Jan 18th. – This morning having safely embarked the sealskins I settled with Mr Hansen. We started first to look for some reefs he mentioned as not being marked on the chart, and then on to Keppel Island, the headquarters of the Tierra del Fuegian and Patagonian Mission. We found Mr Hansen's information as to the rocks correct, so I shall warn the Hydrographic Office. We passed Saunders Island, on which is the site of the first settlement; a few of the ruined walls are still standing. We then anchored in Committee Bay, Keppel Island, at the head of which is the Mission.

The history of this organisation is a saga of missionary perseverance in the face of almost every imaginable disaster. The Patagonian Missionary Society had been founded by Commander Allen Gardiner R.N. in 1844. Gardiner was a zealous evangelist, who had retired from the navy at the age of 32 in order to devote his life to missionary work. After three failed attempts to establish missions in remote parts of Africa and South America, he finally persuaded six other men to accompany him to Tierra del Fuego, but they all starved to death on the shores of the Beagle Channel in 1851, fleeing from the hostility of the Indians whose souls they had come to save.

Examination of the seamanship aspects of this gruesome story leaves one with a suspicion that Commander Gardiner's conduct amounted to something close to self-imposed martyrdom. His wilful persistence in ignoring the dangers of the enterprise led to accusations of fanaticism, but the drama and tragedy of his fate struck a chord that reverberated loudly in Victorian England, and donations to the Patagonian Mission began to flow. By 1855 the organisers were in a position to establish a base on Keppel Island from which to continue Gardiner's work. Their plan was to use a schooner, to be named the Allen Gardiner, *to ship a few Indians at a time from Tierra del Fuego to Keppel, where they would live for some months*

"We anchored in Committee Bay, Keppel Island, at the head of which is the Mission..." (page 117)

Photo: Jane Cameron

The settlement buildings can be seen in the centre of the picture. The Mission Station was established in 1855 by the Patagonian Missionary Society, and operated until 1898. It was then run as a farm until 1911, when the island was sold to Dean Brothers. Now in private ownership, Keppel was a sheep farm until 1992, and today is uninhabited.

118

"They all starved to death on the shores of the Beagle Channel..." (page 117)

This drawing appeared in *The Illustrated London News* of 8 May 1852, and shows a party from H.M.S. *Dido* (Captain Moorshead) discovering the remains of Commander Gardiner's catechist, Mr Maidment, in a cave. Captain Moorshead's narrative, described as "painfully interesting", was also published. The consequent huge publicity generated criticism of Commander Gardiner's rashness, admiration for his martyrdom, and support for his cause.

learning the rudiments of civilised behaviour, farming, and above all Christianity. Then they would be returned to their homes to set a good example to their brethren. They would be taught English, and the missionaries would in turn learn their language, and thus God's word would spread among the "poor benighted Fuegians," as one of the mission wives called them.

This plan created incomprehension and misunderstanding on both sides. An example of the lesser consequences of this is enshrined in today's Admiralty Chart of the area, where a certain Sound is called "Tekenika," the Yaghan word for "I don't understand what you mean" – clearly a response to the question "What do you call this place?" But more serious results of mutual misunderstanding showed themselves. The missionaries, their attitude typical of the day, regarded the Indians as degraded savages, in need of rescue. Even more extreme ignorance and prejudice is shown by the German photographer Gustav Schultz who asserts that Yaghans "eat their wives and mothers-in-law when pressed by hunger" and "drown their children if too tired to carry them along."

In fact the Yaghans possessed a sophisticated language, amazing hardiness, and a social structure well designed to cope with their very harsh environment. Their resentment at what must have seemed a totally unwarranted threat to their way of life erupted in a further catastrophe. In 1859 the missionaries built a little church at Woollya in Tierra del Fuego, but during the singing of the dedicatory hymn the congregation was attacked by Yaghans with clubs and spears, and slaughtered to a man. Only the ship's cook survived to tell the awful tale; he had been left on board the schooner as watchman, and leapt overboard to swim for his life when the Yaghans came for him.

Many people were by this time questioning the wisdom of the whole enterprise, and the methods being used. The Governor of the Falkland Islands decided to hold an official enquiry, with which the missionaries refused to co-operate. William Parker Snow, the first captain of the mission schooner, spoke of "the natives being brought to (Keppel) island and under the plea of teaching them made to work and attend upon the party."[44] He noted the reluctance of the Indians to leave their homeland and visit Keppel, and likened the operation to the Slave Trade. Although his views were

[44]Statement to the Stanley Court by W.P. Snow 22 September 1856.

coloured by a fierce quarrel with Despard, the head of the mission, he was not alone in his criticisms.

In a report to the Secretary of State on the Woollya massacre, Governor Moore wrote that he did not think "that the natives were contented with their enforced residence at Keppel."[45] At the official enquiry the Fuegian Jemmy Button testified in his broken English, "I stayed at Keppel Island four moons with wife and children – did not like to stop – don't want to – don't like it."

The Register of Deaths shows a high Yaghan mortality on Keppel Island. The average age of death was nineteen, and the causes given are chiefly influenza and breathing ailments. And one entry that records the death of Muthunger, an eleven-year-old labourer, makes one wonder exactly what was going on.

All criticism was hotly disputed by Despard, who maintained that the Indians had all come to Keppel of their own free will, and had been treated there with great kindness. Nonetheless, Governor Moore decreed that no more Indians were to be brought over until the missionaries could clear themselves of "the grave suspicions which have become current in the Colony regarding their dealings with the natives." In giving his views on the situation he wrote to the Duke of Newcastle, then Secretary of State for the Colonies, "I submit to your Grace that it is practically impossible for Mr Despard or his agents, only acquainted with a few words of the language of one tribe, to make a contract which could for a moment be considered equal or fair with the savages." In a later dispatch he continued, "I do not intend to cast the slightest reflection on the objects or intentions of the Mission. I believe their enterprise to be a pure and holy one. But however great may be the prospective advantages to the Fuegians from residence and instruction in the Falkland Islands, I cannot consent to them being deported hither from their own land without their consent, a consent moreover that must be given in a knowledge of the character and duration of their proposed residence."

Victorian missionaries never abandoned the task that God had entrusted to them, and set-backs were seen as new challenges. They eventually managed to reassure the Government that undue pressure would not be exerted on the Fuegians, and operations were resumed. But it was not until

[45]This and subsequent quotations are taken from "Despatches to the Secretary of State 1860" Nos. 10-28. Jemmy Button's verbatim evidence was attached in one of the many supporting documents.

121

Thomas Bridges, Despard's adopted son, had taught himself the Yaghan language that real progress became possible. Bridges paved the way for the final establishment of a mission station in Tierra del Fuego, of which he took over the running in 1871.

By the time of Dwarf's *visit, the new station at Ushuaia and the base at Keppel were running in tandem, with a mixed degree of success which Wiseman was to record with his usual perceptiveness.*

I landed in the afternoon and was received by Mr Bartlett the farm manager, a jolly old English farmer, and Mr Barley[46] the catechist, a very missionary-looking party. Up we went to Mr Bartlett's house, quite like a clean, well-to-do farmhouse in England, and I was introduced to his wife and daughters, all very nice civil people. They persuaded me to stay to tea and we had all sorts of home-made luxuries: brawn, pasties and no end of gooseberry tart (fresh gooseberries out of the garden). Altogether I enjoyed myself and spoiled my dinner. At seven I bade farewell to my kind hosts, having previously invited them on board to see the gun drill on Friday. Tomorrow I go out for a shoot.

Jan 19th. – My friend Mrs Bartlett sent me off a jug of the most delicious cream I ever saw out of Devonshire, better even than the Carcass first-class production. After luncheon I landed with the Doctor and Seymour to shoot. The island is alive with rabbits, but they are very wild and have such a lot of holes that the only chance of getting them is early in the morning or late at night. We spread out and walked up a valley that leads to some ponds in hopes of getting a few unwary bunnies, but the result was only one to Seymour's gun. On arrival at the water we saw a lot of grebe, but could not get the beasts, they are so wary and dive so quickly. I spent nearly the whole afternoon lying under a tussac bog waiting to get a shot at the little varmints but to no purpose. The consequence was when we mustered to walk back my share of the bag consisted of only a teal. It was now getting well towards the evening

[46]Leonard Burleigh worked for sixteen years with the Feugian Indians, first on Keppel Island, and later on the remote Woolaston Islands near Cape Horn, where he and his wife Ellen, with tremendous courage, established a branch of the Patagonian Mission. They seemed to be succeeding in an almost impossible situation after many hardships when Burleigh was drowned in 1894, knocked overboard by the boom while out sailing alone.

"Quite like a clean, well-to-do farmhouse in England..." (page 122)

The stone house on Keppel Island, uninhabited for some years. The only other Mission building to survive intact is the chapel, which has been extended and adapted for use as a shearing shed. The substantial ruins of other structures can still be seen around the settlement.

Photo: Jane Cameron

123

so we spread out for bunnies again and managed to get ten between us by the time we got down to the boat.

Jan 20th. – This was a most wonderful day and will take a deal of describing. At half past ten I sent a boat in for the good people, and in due time arrived the Bartlett family consisting of Père et Mère and the two daughters, nice, fresh neat-looking girls evidently well brought up, in fact the whole family a very good specimen of the small yeoman farmer at home. Then Mr and Mrs Barley with a big ugly baby that looked as if it was suffering from water on the brain, and a Mrs Willis (wife of the Captain of the mission schooner *Allen Gardiner*[47] now at Tierra del Fuego), with her son a boy of seven or eight years old.

Hardly had they got on board when off came a boat with all the Tierra del Fuegians whom I had given permission to come and see the fun. They are a very unintellectual-looking set with flat coarse features, straight coarse black hair and large heads. Of course they were all dressed in European corduroys and hobnailed boots so perhaps they did not show to advantage; they were certainly not picturesque. Mr Barley told me they have no numeral above four in their language, and any number above that was an indefinite idea expressed by the general term "a large quantity." The missionaries have great difficulty in instilling into their minds the difference between meum and tuum, otherwise they are harmless enough. Only young men are brought here to learn farming and then they are sent back with a few head of cattle to start up near the mission station on Tierra del Fuego.

At first the Mission tried having a school for the girls as well here, but the untutored savage could not be made to see that there was any harm in following the national custom in the matter of wives, that is that they change wives with one another occasionally, just to have a few new ideas, but as you can imagine the shock to propriety was rather dreadful when after educating the good people for some time and marrying some couples they found that the gentle savages had changed wives all round.

[47]Captain J.C.T. Willis was always regarded with great affection and gratitude by Thomas Bridges, to whom in 1886 he lent his life savings to help establish Harberton, the refuge for many years for persecuted Indians. After the Mission moved completely to Ushuaia in 1898, Willis continued to sail coastal schooners around the Falklands. He drowned in rather mysterious circumstances at Punta Arenas in 1908.

"Dressed in European corduroys and hobnailed boots..." (page 124)

For forty years the Mission Station on Keppel Island acted as a temporary home and training centre for the Indians of Tierra del Fuego, mainly Yaghans or Fish Indians as they were known, although some Ona and Tehuelche Indians from further north also seem to have spent time there. The intention was that, having received an education in Christian principles and training in farming and gardening, they should return to Tierra del Fuego to spread Christianity and civilisation among their compatriots.

With hindsight it is not difficult to see why these laudable aims were doomed, in spite of some short-term successes. Eventually disease and a programme of extermination by Argentine settlers drove the natives almost to extinction. Today only a handful of pure-blooded Indians survive.

Photo: J. Goodhart, with kind permission of Commander G.A. Goodhart.

125

So the Mission had to re-sort them and pack the loving couples off to their own country.

Luscombe was also observing, with a slightly cynical eye, the effects of the missionaries' attempts to civilise the Indians: "We steamed on to Keppel Island where there is a mission station for converting the Fuegians: a farmer named Bartlett keeps sheep on the island and a catechist is supported by the Missionary Society to convert these ruffians into Christians, or workmen, whichever pays best. On the 20th all the people came on board and witnessed the men at General Quarter etc. — remaining to lunch: I landed at 4 p.m. and spent the evening at the Bartletts, tuning their piano and talking to the two Miss Bs — one of whom is pretty. I also was shown all over the Mission arrangements; the Fuegians about 20 in number live in two cottages, and work the whole of the island: they are taught to read and write two hours a day, and then they work at the potato gardens, sheep shearing etc. In appearance they are a diminutive, brownish and ugly lot, something between a red Indian and a Chinaman: some of them are quick at learning and can write pretty well: their language is called "Jahlang": they have only 4 numbers, beyond that they can't count. The Mission is managed by the Bishop of the Falklands, and there is a station in Tierra del Fuego, and a schooner runs between, taking back converts (or others)."

The Keppel Mission continued to function much as at the time of Wiseman's visit for another sixteen years, but as the new station at Ushuaia became better established any justification for bringing Indians to the Falklands ceased to exist, and in 1898 the Mission withdrew entirely from Keppel, leaving the island to function simply as a farm. In Tierra del Fuego, meanwhile, the Revd. Thomas Bridges had broken with the South American Missionary Society, but continued with his family to live among the Indians in their own country, learn their languages, and win their confidence to a degree that had been impossible before. Bridges watched with horror the southward advance of Argentine settlers, who regarded the Indians as vermin and paid a bounty for each one shot. He and his family made every effort to protect them, establishing farms first at Harberton, then at Viamonte, where the Indians could live and work unmolested.

Sadly, in the end, all the efforts of both the Mission and the Bridges family proved in vain. By 1930 the native Indians of Tierra del Fuego had become all but extinct, devastated by measles epidemics as well as the

deliberate policy of extermination. Today probably fewer than ten pure-
blooded Indians are the sole survivors of the tribes on whose behalf so much
energy was expended, so much life lost.

But to return to my party. We went to gun drill and all drills connected therewith, at which the ladies were much delighted and the noble savage much bewildered. Then I took them (the ladies) round the ship, after which we had a sort of scramble lunch, the wardroom officers coming in and helping me to entertain my guests; twelve sat down and the rest of us helped wait.

We heard that a Mr Holmested and his wife had come over from the main on purpose to see the Doctor, so I sent in to the settlement for them and they arrived just in time to sit down with my second batch. He is an Essex man from Braintree, I believe his father was a doctor there and afterwards in London, she was a Miss Davis, daughter of a London doctor. They had a baby boy with them. Fancy, they came over in a little dinghy, nine miles. I found them both very pleasant people indeed. The husband is a large proprietor on West Falklands, he and his partner having some 25,000 sheep between them. I pitied her, poor thing, no lady within fifteen miles of her and only one woman in her husband's settlement, the wife of a shepherd. No doctor on the island at all, in fact it would take at least a week ere a doctor could be got at in case of necessity.

After lunch we all adjourned to the wardroom where the piano was got under way, and Seymour sang a lot of songs. Then we got Mrs Holmested to play, which she did rather well, but her singing was a failure. At about four all the people landed having I think thoroughly enjoyed their outing.

I landed with the Doctor and the Paymaster to ride out to a penguin rookery where there were also Mollymauks as I wanted a specimen. Mr Bartlett who accompanied us had the horses ready and off we started. After an hour's ride over the camp we came to the place and went down to pick out a victim; it seemed very cruel, the birds were so tame they would hardly get out of your way, and the young ones, large balls of grey fluff, were sitting up in their nests snapping at you with their long beaks. However as we had come all that way to get a specimen I hardened my heart, picked out an old gentleman who appeared to be a

"I found them both very pleasant people indeed..." (page 127)

The son of an Essex doctor, eager to travel the world in search of adventure, Ernest Holmested had arrived in the Falklands in 1868. He farmed at Shallow Bay, initially in partnership with William Wickham Bertrand, and later with Robert Blake. In 1880 he married Edith Davies, daughter of a Hampstead doctor, and brought her back to the Islands. They returned to live in England ten years later, although Holmested continued in financial partnership with Blake at Hill Cove.

Photo: with kind permission of Miss Betty Stronach

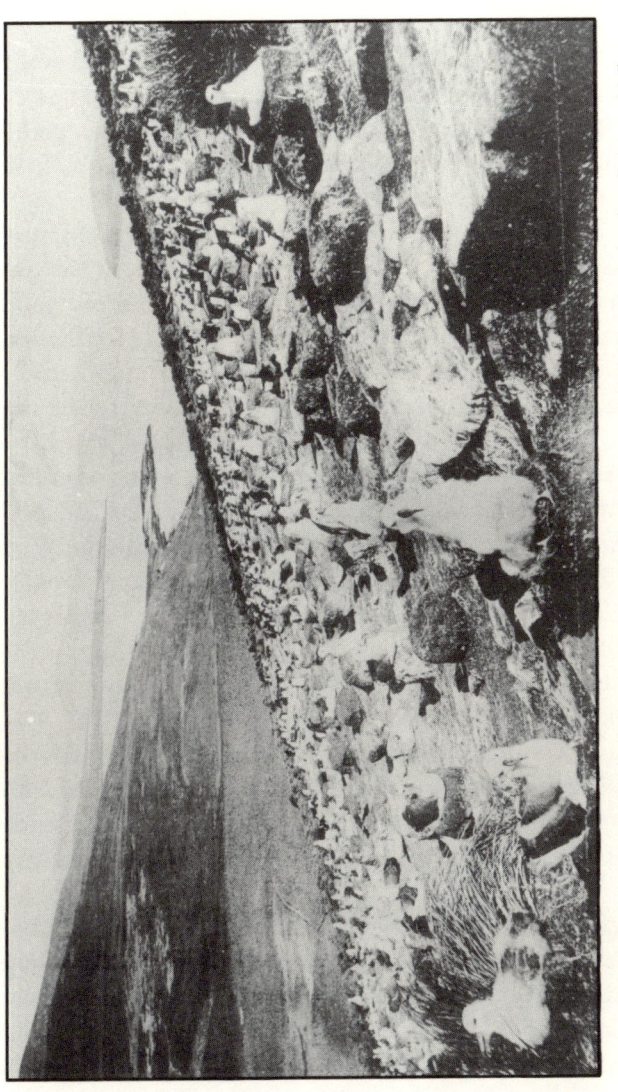

"Large balls of grey fluff, sitting up in their nests snapping at you with their long beaks..." (page 127)

A Mollymauk rookery on West Falkland. Mollymauk is the local name for the Black-Browed Albatross (*Diomedea melanophris*). Their nests are constructed as pillars of mud and grass, placed some distance apart from each other on sloping ground, which enables the birds with their huge wingspan to take off more easily. A chick, the "large ball of grey fluff" described by Wiseman, sits in the lower centre of the picture. Mollymauk eggs were once a popular item of food in the Islands, although rarely eaten today.

Photo: *Wiseman Collection*

129

bachelor with no family to support, and I knocked him over and took his head and wings as a trophy which you will I hope see and admire. The wings measure three foot four inches each, and his entire spread was seven foot two.

Home we rode and very heavy I found my trophies and glad was I once more to alight at Mrs Bartlett's hospitable door. She had some tea ready for us and was so kind as to give me some lovely brown grebe skins, also some robins' breasts and the breast of a lovely pink gull, these were to be taken home carefully for "My Lady".

I bade adieu to our kind hosts and hurried off, having asked Mr and Mrs Holmested to dinner and Seymour to meet them. A very pleasant evening was the result; by the bye Mrs H. gave me the address of a good furrier which I enclose in case you have not got one in mind for the seal skins. Our friends went ashore about eleven and are to start back tomorrow in their dinghy – poor woman she came all this way to see the Doctor.

Jan 21st. – We started at 8 a.m. for Pebble Island. Just before we sailed I received a sea-otter skin and a little Tierra del Fuegian basket and shell necklace, so you see Winnie is not forgotten. We got through the West Channel safely and anchored off Pebble Island settlement about noon. It was blowing so hard that I did not send a boat in shore, but I employed the afternoon with the Doctor in curing Molly's head and wings.

Jan 22nd. – A lovely day but still blowing. Mr Charles Dean[48] who is farming this island came off to church, and we had hymns no. 223, 406, 365. The Epistle as you will know was taken from one of your favourite chapters. In the evening we had Service on deck. Mr Dean lunched with me, but I did not venture on shore although he tried hard to persuade me, the weather is so unsettled that I fear a heavy blow, good night dear wife.

Jan 23rd. – Happy to say our fine weather has not deserted us, and so at 9 a.m. the Doctor, Luscombe, Horwill and self landed to breakfast with Mr Dean and then shoot. It has been a perfect day, quite like bright summer weather at home. Mr Dean has quite a comfortable house built of wood, it was sent out from England with furniture to suit. After a

[48]Charles Montague Dean was the younger brother of George Markham Dean,
   Wiseman's acquaintance from Stanley. Pebble Island is still owned by Dean Bros.
   although none of the family now live in the Falklands.

capital breakfast we started out on horseback for our shoot. There were any number of teal and duck and in a short time I had shot about a dozen of the former, and by great luck managed to get another silver grebe.

Mr Dean and myself then left the rest of the party as I wanted to go and have a look at Tamar Pass through which we have to go tomorrow. This was another hour's ride during which we came across a good many sheep cast. One poor beast had one eye picked out by the Johnny Rooks[49] (a sort of kite) which are always hovering about to attack wounded or dying animals. The poor sheep was still alive but very weak. We got it to lie down comfortably and Mr Dean said he would send a man out to look after it as soon as we returned.

We rode on to Tamar Pass and although the channel is straight it is not a very inviting-looking place, especially with the tide running through as it was then, like a mill race. However if it is fine I shall try it at slack water tomorrow. Coming back we had some great sport with wild goslings, just before they are able to fly. We coursed them on horseback and after a time they hid in the long grass when you mark them down and catch them. This is rather difficult as they hide so close you may almost tread on them without seeing them. We picked up the rest of the party at the ponds, they having shot any quantity of teal, and started for home.

Mr Dean came off to dinner with me and I had the Doctor to meet him. I was presented with a very handsome wild goat's head shot on this island[50].

Jan 24th. – Having said goodbye to Mr Dean we started for Port Sussex in hopes of getting mail. The Tamar Pass was successfully got through, but I must confess to being very glad when we were clear of it. It is not a pleasant sensation to be going for three miles through a narrow

[49]Johnny Rook is the local name for the Striated Caracara (*Phalcoboenus australis*), a rare species restricted to a few South Atlantic islands. However it is fairly common in certain parts of the Falklands, especially on the West, and is a fearless scavenger, regarded as a pest by some farmers.

[50]Luscombe observed that there were 2,600 sheep and 500 wild cattle on Pebble Island, which was run by a total of two men. Today there are over 12,000 sheep, and domestic cattle only, but the workforce has remained about the same: normally three, but occasionally four, men. Goats, like the pigs, rabbits and hares running wild elsewhere in the Islands, would have been originally imported by sealers as a renewable source of food. Today the feral pigs and goats have been eliminated throughout the Falklands.

"We started out on horseback..." (page 131)

George Dean, son of Wiseman's host on Pebble Island, and nephew of the hospitable Mrs Dean of Stanley. He is riding without the normal Falkland Island saddle-covering of a cojinilla (sheepskin; pronounced "cockineesha") – one of the many words connected with riding, which along with place names are a legacy of the Uruguayan gauchos of the nineteenth century, and still in use in the Islands today.

Photo: Falkland Islands Museum

132

channel with the tide running like a race and rocks on either side, knowing that if the man at the helm mistakes your order or anything breaks down the ship must inevitably go on the rocks and most likely stay there[51]. However "all's well that ends well," and we got safely through.

We arrived at Port Sussex about five o'clock, when to my disgust there was only a letter from Mr Cobb telling me the mail had not arrived – when shall I get news of my dear wife, I do long for it so. As there were no mails I determined to go on to Port Howard, where we arrived at nine o'clock just saving the daylight. It is a wonderful harbour, you go steaming apparently right up against a cliff when all of a sudden a little opening shows and you pass through into a perfectly land-locked harbour.

Jan 25th. – I find *Garnet* has been here with our mails and has left for Fox Bay and Stanley, so I shall be after her like a shot as soon as we can get away. I should have started this morning but unfortunately there is a little repair wanted in the engine which will take until tomorrow evening, so I shall not be able to start until Friday morning in pursuit. At any rate it is a satisfaction to know where our mails are and that we shall have them in another three days. It is raining hard so I shall not see much of Port Howard this day.

I stood it up to four o'clock and then in desperation sent to ask the Doctor whether he would come for a walk in the rain with me. He agreed so off we went, landing abreast the ship. We tramped up to the settlement through what struck us as the longest and wettest grass we had ever seen. Once there however we got a good hour's stretch, and at the end a hearty welcome from Mr Waldron the owner of this part of the country, who promised us a good day's fishing tomorrow, and if I will stay a day's wild bull stalking the next day. He returned to the ship with us and dined with me. I have got four more otter skins for my wife, and will now say goodnight, God bless her.

Jan 26th. – About 9 o'clock the Doctor and I started off on horseback with a guide for our day's fishing, the river being some nine miles away up in the hills. After a pleasant ride through very fine grassland we came to a very likely-looking trout stream and set to work. It was not long ere

[51]Luscombe states that this three miles took 40 minutes at full speed, the ship making about 8 knots through the water.

133

"I determined to go on to Port Howard..." (page 133)

This contemporary photograph shows the manager's house on the spot where the present manager lives. During *Dwarf*'s visit one of the ship's officers wrote in his journal that shearing was in progress, that the estate had 40,000 sheep, and that one man could hand-shear about 60 sheep a day.

Today the Port Howard estate carries 46,000 sheep on its 220,000 acres, and shearing is done largely by teams of contract shearers, each man machine-shearing 200–300 sheep a day.

Photo: Wiseman Collection

we scored each a brace of fish, but after that not a rise was to be got for love or fly, so we dismissed our sandwiches and smoked in peace for some time whilst our guide, who had been joined by two shepherds, proceeded to roast a gosling we had knocked over. It was most interesting to watch the different sorts of wild fowl in the stream for there were quantity of teal, widgeon, grey duck and upland goose, and had we brought our guns we could have shot any number of them.

After our pipes we set to work again and after about three hours managed to muster seven brace and a half of fish between us. The fish are something like our trout in shape and size but have no scabs or red spots. But the rest of their colouring is like our fish, and they are excellent eating[52]. We were assured by our guide that had it been a good day we should have caught twenty or thirty brace. The weather certainly was not in the most favourable condition, it having rained heavily the night before, which not only raised the water but turned it to the colour of pea-soup.

On our return to the settlement Mr Waldron insisted on our staying to dinner, when we met his brother who had just arrived from England and come in from Stanley in the mail schooner bringing news up to the 10th December. How I envied the people their letters. I heard today that *Garnet* has gone to Port Stephens so I shall not start until Saturday.

Jan 27th. – It is blowing a gale from the S.W. so here we are stuck, and consequently the Doctor and self left the ship at 7 a.m. on bull-shooting intent. Oh, what a glorious day we had! Please dismiss from your mind the day at West Point Island, that was just child's play; the cattle there were, as compared with what we saw today, tame and quiet. But to tell you the yarn properly I must begin at the beginning. Mr Waldron kindly sent his Capitaz, an Englishman, to show us the sport. He is the head man who breaks in the horses and lassoes the wild cattle. Having strapped our rifles under the sheepskins of the native saddles off we then started, at a pretty sharp pace as we had twenty-eight miles to ride out to the ground. The first ten or twelve miles was over very good grass camp well watered. We crossed three good-sized streams, one

[52]The Falkland Trout (*Aplochiton zebra*) was once fairly common in streams and rivers, but numbers declined after the introduction, in the middle of this century, of Brown Trout (*Salmo trutta*), which flourished immediately, and swiftly took over the habitat of the smaller native species in all but a few rivers and lakes.

quite as large as the Don at Glenkindie. After this we got into very rough boggy ground with big tufted grass, and it was precious hard to keep up with the good Capitaz who went along at a hard gallop. At last we saw a shepherd's hut in the distance and beyond some high mountains.

"This is your ground" said our friend, "and in half an hour you must begin to look out for game." At the end of that time he halted and got the rifles out whilst we tightened up the girths and listened to his words of wisdom: "You see, Captain, these beasts are very wild and so you must be ready as soon as you have fired to jump on the horse and ride off, as if you do not knock him over he will charge you. I will head any bull we pick out. You gentlemen must ride close up with me, and as soon as he stands, jump off and fire and up again. One thing more: do not get below the bull but always on higher ground. If you let him get above you and he charges you will have but a poor chance of getting away. Mind gentlemen, I will do all I can to get the bulls to stand, but after that it must depend on yourselves. You must be steady and not fire until you are sure. For I warn you they are very wicked animals, and being constantly hunted and harassed are very savage when they see horsemen."

With these useful hints, a sandwich and a pull at the flask, we mounted and rode on. It was not long however before we saw a great white bull some five hundred yards away in a hollow. He appeared a little lame but trotted off pretty well on seeing us. "Follow me" shouted the Capitaz, and off we started at full gallop. It was quite as much as we could do to keep up, what with the rough country and a heavy ship's rifle to carry into the bargain. We soon closed with our friend the bull who, as soon as he saw he was being overtaken, turned and began pawing the ground and shaking his great head at us, for he was a magnificent fellow. "Get above him, ride close up and fire," called out our guide, "I will turn him." He then rode across in front of the bull shouting, when the old gentleman turned and made a short dash in his direction looking round at us occasionally, rather puzzled as to whom he should go for. We are within range, so off I jump and fire, up again to find I had only hit him high in the fleshy part of the shoulder and that he intends a go at me. Luckily the Doctor is close to, and with a splendid shot behind the shoulder brings our friend down. We ride up and find him a grand beast, one of the largest bulls I think I ever saw.

I should tell you the sheep farmers are very anxious to get rid of all wild cattle as they do not pay and take up ground that would feed sheep. Soon we see a herd of a dozen down by a little mountain stream half a mile away. There is not much cover but we ride off towards the Capitaz, who is waving frantically and has headed three bulls off. We go as hard as we can, and presently come up to him just as one of the beasts has turned, and evidently means mischief. "Take care and mind you shoot straight," says our guide. "This bull has someone's lasso on him and will charge, for he is a saucy one." We ride up and get within about thirty yards of him, and with a lucky shot I drop him just as he makes a dash at the Capitaz. Up we jump and after the other two, the first of which after charging all of us in turn, and I confess getting much too near me to be pleasant, is dropped by the Doctor. The third falls to me and we call a halt for a pipe and a rest. This is hard work I can tell you.

After a spell we start off again for another bull, who turns and goes for us as soon as we get near. He charges us all as we are together, and off we go in different directions to wheel up again as soon as he stops. The Doctor fires, hits him but not fatally, and he charges right for the Doctor. It is a critical moment, I cannot fire for fear of hitting the Capitaz who is just opposite, and the Doctor's horse refuses to move. On comes the bull, and I just make up my mind to wait until he gets close and fire at all hazards when the Capitaz pluckily dashes in between the bull and his intended victim. It is a close thing, the bull turns and his horn is within a foot of the Capitaz's horse. Luckily they come past me and I am able to bowl my friend over for he is not ten yards away, and he falls just clear of the horse. He was a grand fellow, dun-coloured with enormous breadth between his horns and such a chest; he regularly shook the ground when he fell. I should very much like to have his head and horns but the distance is very great and we have no saw to cut them out, so I must leave him with the rest to be skinned by the men tomorrow, but shall try and get Mr Waldron to secure his horns for me.

After mutual congratulations on our escapes we ride on. I was very nervous about the Doctor and certainly the Capitaz saved his life.

We found no more bulls in our path, and rode on to a shepherd's hut where we were regaled with tea and fresh trout out of the river. The men went out to get us fresh horses, and after half an hour's rest away we went. Oh how rough and bad the ground seemed, and what an abomi-

"We rested once at the house of another shepherd whose wife gave us a drink of milk..." (page 139)

This photograph, taken on West Falkland, is probably of the Halliday family. Shepherds' wives had to cope with a demanding and self-sufficient existence, bringing up large families in small houses, with the nearest neighbour often many hours' ride away.

Photo: J. Goodhart, with kind permission of Commander G.A. Goodhart

nation the South American saddle[53] and how I longed for an English one. I pushed on at a canter which was a deal more comfortable. We rested once at the house of another shepherd whose wife gave us a drink of milk, and on again. How long the way seemed! I noticed no one was much given to talking during our return journey, and as I looked at the Doctor I saw a sort of resigned, hopeless expression upon his face and felt it was but a reflection of my own.

However all things must come to an end and at last this ride did. How thankfully we tumbled into the boat, not, however, before thanking our host Mr Waldron and the Capitaz for the best day's sport I ever had in my life, notwithstanding the fifty mile ride.

Jan 28th. – Blowing a gale, so I fear we shall not get away until Sunday. The Doctor comes up to report the sick and we compare notes: both very stiff, and feel as if we had ridden a hundred and fifty miles instead of fifty yesterday, but still agree that it was the best day's sport we ever had. In fact I find myself talking bulls to everyone patient enough to listen. In the evening I landed to say goodbye to Mr Waldron and picked up some very good fossils, so you see my collection is growing, all for my wife.

[53]These may either have been the padded leather sections, laced together down the centre, known as *bastoos*, or the wooden-framed saddle known as the Falkland Island saddle, or *malvinero*, both originating with the Uruguayan gauchos. However they are both comfortable to ride on when covered, as is usual, by the *cojinilla*, or sheepskin.

Lady Wiseman, née Elizabeth Langworthy, had been married to Sir William for three years at the time of these letters, and had produced two daughters. A son was born three years later.

Photo: Wiseman Collection

CHAPTER 9

BACK TO STANLEY

Jan 29th. – A lovely morning and we are off at 4 a.m. and across to Port Sussex, as a mail may by this time have arrived.

Much to our disappointment the only thing there is a letter from Cobb telling me that the mail is all addressed *Garnet*, so I must wait until we arrive at Stanley. Such a lovely evening and fine night with bright moon, these particulars I had ample opportunity of studying, being on deck most the night as we coasted along.

Jan 30th. – Arrived at Stanley at six in the morning and having opened the mails I got your dear letter No. 4. The *Garnet* has got the others. Dear wife, I must devote another page to the answering of your letter, or rather begin afresh. I hope you will not have been wearied by this long egotistical account of our trip, but perhaps you may find something of interest. At any rate you have the full account of all our doings. It was a very pleasant cruise, but how I missed you, you would have taken so much interest in seeing this strange country and admiring the wild rugged beauty of its coasts.

Meanwhile, back home at The Grange, Lady Wiseman was recovering her health after a difficult birth and keeping the home fires burning. She wrote to her husband in terms which will seem familiar to many naval families:

"What a tossing you must have had. I know you will think me silly, but I get so frightened when the wind gets up. Do be careful because a chill in that weather would make you so ill. I wonder if there is a good doctor on board the Dwarf...

"I am not (as your mother says) accustomed to Naval Separation, and God grant I may never get accustomed to it if it means indifference to your being away...

"I have been out driving today in my little phaeton for half an hour, and have not needed a visit by the doctor for five days. James (the footman) asked

all about you. Carry and Winnie occupied the back seat. But I try not to do too much at present as it is only three weeks since baby was born...

"It is very dreadful, dear Willie, but they tell me Mr Wedemeyer has run away with a married lady. I shall no doubt hear more particulars from Donald or Annie...

"Leaving the opera we had a horrid bother with the cabman who after driving us a few minutes landed us opposite a public house and refused to take us further. Fortunately a policeman found us another cab, and I took the man's number and the policeman's and have written about him...

"If you are able to get some seal skins they would be very useful and I should like them very much. They are such expensive things to buy in England...

"I have had to give Mrs Martin notice for she cannot wash at all...

"One of the geese was killed on the day of the christening for the servants, and very good and fat it was...

"I spent a very pleasant evening with the Watsons and we went to the Criterion to see "Foggerty's Fairy", a play written by Gilbert, but not a success. Mrs Langtry has taken to the stage...

"There are four commanders promoted I see, but as my new Navy List has not yet arrived I cannot tell whether they are junior to you. But Captain Paul says your promotion must come soon. How I look forward to that, and all our present separation ended. I am so glad you like the Dwarf officers, and the people seem so pleasant...

"I am anxiously awaiting for the middle of April and then I may reasonably hope their Lordships at the Admiralty will make up their minds – if they have any – what is to become of the Dwarf...

"If you stay out any longer than June I shall come out to you. I do not mind the journey a bit, and I can leave the children behind. If the Dwarf is recommissioned out abroad I will come as soon as I can manage it. I can stay until your promotion comes and then we can return together. Oh dear! – this waiting while promotions are made; how I hate them all at the Admiralty...

"I must finish my letter now. If only your little wife could put herself in the envelope instead of the letter, and as you open it welcome you with a kiss. But I am afraid she would be too shy to kiss such an important person as the Captain of the Dwarf, and must wait till he becomes once more the Commander of The Grange."

Jan 31st. – My own dear wife, how happy your letters have made me (for in the *Garnet* this afternoon I received Nos. 1, 2 and 3). I was so longing to hear of you. I shall wait until we get to sea to answer all your questions, as now with Capn. Jones always wanting me for some business or other I hardly have a moment to myself. It is very flattering that he should ask my opinion, still I would much rather he left me alone. Capn. Packe has kindly asked me to stay with him, so I shall remove there today and get my cabin cleaned properly. The Dwarfs are to dine at Dean's this evening, a big dinner of which you shall have a description later on.

Feb 1st. – This morning I went down to Mr Cobb and arranged to have the seal skins sent home from here by sailing ship well packed. Mr Cobb has had lots dressed in England and will give me the name of a good man. He says you must be very careful that they do not cheat you and send back other skins instead of your own, so you must look out for the wily furrier. Then again they try and keep back all the bits cut off which will make gloves, bags etc. but you must make them give them up. I have sent eight skins; you should have them dressed and then select the best for a jacket. I believe it takes five or six skins to make a good jacket. I will from Monte Video send you the sea-otter skins.

Oh, such a long, tiresome dinner we had – the Governor and Mrs Kerr, Mr and Mrs Cobb, Capn. Packe and four of our people, the Doctor, Luscombe, Hamm and Webb. The only amusing incident was Capn. Packe's constantly contradicting whatever the Governor said in the driest way possible.

The day has been wretched. You are naughty, your first letter dated Nov. 6th was not numbered, and I have been in a fit thinking a letter was missing and worried Capn. Jones' life out about it. Of course looking carefully at the dates I saw my mistake.

Mr Dean has undertaken to send you two guanaco and two ostrich rugs. They will come in his ship the *Dennis Brundrit*[54].

Feb 2nd. – A fine day but I got stuck on board the *Garnet* all day today. I did not get away until four o'clock and had, instead of going for

[54]A 563 ton barque, she arrived in the Islands in a parlous state in 1879, and was condemned. She was purchased by J.M. Dean and Co. and repaired, running for seven years between London and Stanley. She was finally wrecked at the entrance to Salvador waters in 1892. A few of her ribs are still visible today in the kelp at low tide.

> *October, 1866,*
> *Thursday 4th*
> *We gave a house warming*
> *Governor & Mrs Robinson, Mr & Mrs*
> *Foster, Dr & Mrs McClinton to dinner,*
> *& every body else invited after,*
> *Bulls I am happy to say*
> *were at Heppel & did not*
> *come, & they were a good*
> *riddance, we had for dinner*
> *Turtle soup, curried kidney,*
> *roast fowls, roast ducks,*
> *boiled leg of mutton, Ham,*
> *chicken pie, stewed steak*
> *& mushrooms, potatoes, peas,*
> *greens, Alma pudding,*
> *malboro pudding, custards,*
> *pink & white blanc mange*
> *dessert, Port, sherry, champagne,*
> *claret, beer. – tea in the drawing –*
> *room, then the gentlemen played*

"The Dwarfs are to dine at Dean's this evening, a big dinner…" (page 143)

Big dinners were clearly Mrs Dean's forte. Fifteen years earlier she described in her diary the modest repast provided for eight people at her house-warming in Stanley Cottage: "Turtle soup, curried kidneys, roast fowls, roast ducks, boiled leg of mutton, ham,

whist in the green house. & we
had music & singing in the
drawing room. I wore my dark
blue silk. — pearl ornaments.
we had supper at ½ past 11..
They left about 2 or 3. ———
weather fine, Summers &
Jane waited, Mrs Hilton helped
to cook, Eliza sent things in
very nicely, Capt Deuxton china
boy cook made the curry. —
everything went off well, &
nothing broken.

———————————
Tuesday 9th —
Pet & I dined at Government
House, with the Baileys, Elliot,
& Mr Byng, I wore my lemon
skirt, black velvet long sleeves
body, pearl ornaments, Pet his
coral studs, we spent a very
pleasant evening. I left about

chicken pie, stewed steak and mushrooms, potatoes, peas, greens, alma pudding, Malbro pudding, custards, pink & white blanc mange, dessert, port, sherry, champagne, claret, beer, - tea in the drawing-room." For those still peckish after the cards and music which followed, "we had supper at ½ past 11."

From the original: John Smith Collection

"Captain Packe has kindly asked me to stay with him so I shall remove there today..." (page 143)

Sir William wrote on the back of this photograph, which he sent to his wife, "The left hand window nearest the outhouse was my bedroom."

The building was known as Sulivan House, and was one of the oldest buildings in Stanley, having been constructed by Captain (later Admiral Sir James) Sulivan in 1844. Sulivan was Fitzroy's Second Lieutenant in the *Beagle*, and became a great friend of Darwin's. After his time in the *Beagle* Sulivan returned to the Islands and carried out some excellent surveying; his name and Fitzroy's are on the Admiralty chart of Stanley (see back endpaper). Sulivan then decided to bring his family to the Falklands and try his hand at farming; his son Falkland Sulivan was the first British subject to be born in the Islands. He later sold the house to Captain Packe. It was destroyed by fire in 1929, and the present Sulivan House, on the same site, was built in 1930 to serve as the Colonial Secretary's (later Chief Executive's) residence. Captain Packe's name survived in the wooden jetty opposite the house, always known as "Packe's Farm Jetty" until it was demolished in 1993.

Photo: Wiseman Collection

146

a walk, to make a lot of calls, and on landing dined at Government House. Present besides the Governor's family were Capn. Jones, the Bishop and Miss Stirling, Packe, Mr and Mrs Dean, Doctor Hamilton[55], Mr Bailey (Police Magistrate), Lieut. Prothero[56] and Mr Norris of *Garnet*. A bad dinner and a dull evening.

Feb 3rd. – Blowing hard all day and raining. Went in the afternoon down to Cobb's to see the photos he has taken, he having kindly promised to give me copies of them. They were very interesting and I shall, as soon as we arrive at Monte Video, send them on to you. He has also promised to shoot the *Dwarf* before we leave[57].

Feb 4th. – Last night our men gave a theatrical entertainment in the little amateur theatre here, I send you the programme. They did very well, and a song between the pieces sung by Mr Seymour was a great success. Everyone in the place that could get room was there, and all passed off well. Today I have a dinner party consisting of the Governor, Bishop, Capn. Jones, Packe, Messrs. Dean and Cobb. So I shall take up my abode on board for the night. The day is fine but bitterly cold.

Feb 5th. – You will be delighted to hear my dinner was a success, all went off well, and so much were they enjoying themselves that it was close upon midnight when we broke up. The Bishop is coming to officiate this forenoon.

His Lordship came and held a Service, Hymns No. 35 Moody and Sankey, A & M Nos. 207, 191. I am sorry to say the sermon had a very soporific effect upon the men. I was much amused at their struggles to keep awake and how one after another they gave in. One man tried hard to keep himself awake by reading the hymn book (not saying much for His Lordship's eloquence) but it was no use. At last even the front row dropped off and their heads sunk placidly on their breasts just under the preacher's nose. This was too much for even a Bishop's equanimity so he

---

[55]Dr Samuel Hamilton was the Colonial Surgeon. Of Irish origin, he had arrived in the Falklands in 1879, and served in his post until his retirement twenty-five years later. Together with Arthur Bailey he signed Mr Horwill's report on Collins.

[56]There were two brothers Prothero in the navy, a competent and undistinguished one called Prothero the Good, and an immensely colourful and terrifying one known to all as Prothero the Bad. This one, who contributed to such a dull evening, must surely have been the Good.

[57]See page 10.

wound up his very uninteresting discourse. After Evening Service I landed, dining and sleeping at Packe's.

Feb 6th. – The *Firefly* arrived today with your letters 6 and 7 together with the Christmas card. Sweetheart, how grieved I am to hear of your remaining weak so long. I do trust your stay at Ellesmere will do you great good and bring strength and health. – I am not going to answer your letters or Winnie's little note until we get to sea.

Feb 7th. – Packe went off early this morning to Fitzroy Harbour and does not return until tomorrow evening when D.V. we shall be on our way to Monte Video. I bade him goodbye hoping we may meet next on the shady side of Pall Mall. I was busy all day arranging about those eternal skins.

Feb 8th. – After bidding adieu to all and getting the photos from Cobb, as well as two pretty white pith frames made by the Misses Kerr out of West Indian pith, I sailed for Monte Video. I am not sorry to get away to a little warmer weather. We anchored for the night in Sparrow Cove.

"This was too much for even a Bishop's equanimity..." (page 147)

The Right Reverend Waite Hockin Stirling was the first Bishop of the Falkland Islands. An energetic and courageous man, he had arrived in the Islands in 1863 as Superintendent of the Mission Station at Keppel. His work with the Indians of Tierra del Fuego led to his appointment as Bishop in 1869. For the next thirty years he administered a huge diocese, which included most of South America, and still found time to initiate and supervise the building of Christ Church Cathedral in Stanley, consecrated in 1892. He retired to England in 1900 and was appointed a Canon of Wells Cathedral, where he remained until his death in 1923. The east window in Christ Church Cathedral commemorates his life and work.

Photo: with kind permission of Mr Alastair Service, Seeley Service and Co. Ltd

Sir William Wiseman was informed of his promotion to Captain when *Dwarf* called at Buenos Aires to collect the mail. Here is a studio portrait of him as a captain wearing his Ceremonial Day Dress with sword and New Zealand medal.

Photo: Wiseman Collection

CHAPTER 10

ROLLING HOME

Feb. 9th. – After a blowy night in Sparrow Cove we started off this morning at seven o'clock and a lovely day we are having. I am going to answer your dear letters on my way up to Monte Video, and I shall take one a day until I have quite exhausted them.

Feb. 10th. – After a dead calm all night, another fine day with little to speak of. I am going to general quarters to fire at a target so shall not be able to add much to my letter this forenoon.

After firing five shots at the target a sudden thick fog came up, so quickly that we nearly lost the target itself. I took a good bearing of him before he disappeared in the fog and by steaming in that direction we came right on it. Of course this stopped our firing so on we went in the thick fog, with steam whistle going hard enough to drive one mad – however we are getting well on our way.

Saturday Feb. 11th. – Now dear wife I am going to answer your letters in detail, to begin yours of Nov 6th. I am so glad the telegram from Vigo cheered you. How well I remember the Easter Sunday you speak of, and how glad I was once more to get my wife downstairs, dear heart we both learnt a lesson by that sad time which I think we shall never forget, it has made us true and lasting friends. Do pray send my best wishes to Annie and Donald on the birth of their child, I hope to hear good accounts of the former by the next mail. I am very glad to hear the girls are going abroad; it will do them a great deal of good and cure Miss Connie of the "Boarding School Miss" style of behaviour. I felt sure Mr and Mrs Lowndes would like to be asked to stand sponsors for little Dolly. We will have our well-earned holiday abroad when *Dwarf* comes home and Their Lordships take it into their heads to promote her captain. Darling, I like the quotation you send me. What is the name of the book? All my energy is directed by that potent spell – "Make your wife have reason to be proud of you."

Dear heart, it is very good of you to send me the Army and Navy

Gazette and I like to see it. Watson is good enough to send me "The Sporting and Dramatic." The Standards interested me very much. Poor Brownrigg, I knew him very well indeed, it is a very sad thing his being killed like that, he leaves a wife and family with, I fear, little to live on.

Your next letter is No. 2 Nov 10th. You poor child, I am very sorry the postal arrangements of Vigo upset you so, to say nothing of the gales. Please thank Sir Henry for the trouble he has taken about my Justiceship, I shall write him by the next mail. I am very glad to hear such good accounts of Frost. In my last I enclosed some seeds of the yellow violet which grows wild in the Falklands, perhaps he will be able to raise some plants; I hope so, as I believe there are few in England. I am also hoping to send some other plants home by the mail, but shall see how they get up to Monte Video. I love to read all your talk about yourself, and know how much you love me. It cannot be more than I love you, bless you, I know full well what a loyal and loving wife you are.

What a dissipation your Christening party, with a big cake! I am disgusted with Mr Hawkins and am equally delighted you have paid him out in the only way he can feel it, viz. via his pocket. Dear wife, you must not think of paying any of my bills, they shall be paid in due course and by me. I should have been more careful and not run up and down from Scotland so often. Your Christmas card I like very much sweetheart, and the loving message written with it still more. I am delighted the conservatory has proved such a success, and hope it will give my wife a great deal of pleasure. I know she will love being able to look after it quite irrespective of the weather and cold. What order it will be in when I get home!

And now sweetheart I shall answer no more letters today but give you a little of our news. We are still steaming with calm weather I am glad to say. It is a little bit an anxious time for me as we have only just enough coal on board to get up to Monte Video, so should head winds prevail we shall be in a bad way as there is no port to put into for coal. However I must hope for the best.

Now to tell you about the photos of the Falkland Islands. I have written the names on the back so that you will know what places they are. No one else can have copies unless given them by Mr Cobb, as there is no public photographer in the islands, so you will have a unique collection.

Feb 12th. – Still fog and northerly winds. I am getting a little anxious about coal, as there is every appearance of a northerly gale. Should that be followed by southerly winds all well and good, but if calms or north winds come after we shall be in a hole. Just now the ship is knocking about and things generally going wrong so I shall lay down my pen.

It is very hard work writing today with the ship wobbling about.

Feb 13th. – I had to give up writing yesterday and on looking at the production I think it is just as well I did. The whole page looks rather as if a fly fresh from the bottom of an ink well had been drying himself on it.

I was awoke this morning about one o'clock by a noise on deck, and the most vivid lightning I ever saw with loud thunder awoke all the wardroom people except Mr Luscombe.

Feb 14th. – Valentine's day and I have nothing to send my dear wife but my best love and that is hers every day. Yesterday turned out a lovely day, pleasant fair breeze and a beautiful calm moonlit night. I went in for sail drill in the afternoon and found the men so fat and lazy from their good living that they could hardly get on the yards, however "nous avons changé tout cela."

Dwarf *reached Montevideo without further incident. Subsequently she was ordered to steam seven hundred miles up the River Parana with the new British Minister of Asunción, the capital of Paraguay, to re-establish diplomatic relations after a breach. No doubt memories of his near-disastrous journey in the* Pioneer *up the Niger came to mind, but this time all went well.*

On returning to Buenos Aires Sir William found in his mail the welcome news of his promotion to captain. This required him to relinquish his brief command and return to England.

His subsequent career looked promising. He commanded a battleship, and seemed destined for Flag rank. However he was struck by pneumonia while sitting on a long court-martial of Vice Admiral Fairfax, who had been partly responsible for the loss of H.M.S. Howe *in Ferrol. He should have reported sick, but this would have required the whole proceedings to have been started again from the beginning, and he held on too long. He died on 11 January 1893, leaving an eight-year-old son to carry on a distinguished name.*

SOURCES AND BIBLIOGRAPHY

Armstrong, Patrick *Darwin's Desolate Islands* (1992)

Barnes, Robert *The Postal Service of the Falkland Islands* (1972)

Boyson, Valentine *The Falkland Islands* (1924)

Bridges, E. Lucas *The Uttermost Part of the Earth* (1948)

British Library Newspaper Library Contemporary newspapers, especially *The Times, The Illustrated Sporting and Dramatic News, The Army and Navy Gazette,* and *The Illustrated London News*

Burke, J. Bernard *A Genealogical and Heraldic Dictionary of the Landed Gentry of Great Britain and Ireland* (1853)

Cawkell, M., Maling, D. and Cawkell, E *The Falkland Islands* (1960)

Clowes, W.L. *The Royal Navy, a History,* vol. VII (1869)

Davies,T.H. and McAdam, J.H. *Wild Flowers of the Falkland Islands* (1989)

Falkland Islands Archives *Despatch and Letter Books 1833–1900; Blue Books of the Colony 1848-1920*

Falkland Islands Government *Registers of Births, Marriages and Deaths 1841–1955; Registers of Shipping 1841–1900*

Falkland Islands Magazine 1892–1933

Hardy, Winona *Bishop Stirling* (1969)

H.M. Stationary Office *Colonial Annual Reports 1870–1900*

Miller, Sydney *A Life of Our Choice* (1989)

Navy Lists 1881 etc.

Parker Snow, William *Memorials* (1858)

Public Record Office, Kew *Ship's logs* ADM53/11677 (1881-1882)

Schulz, Gustav *The Falkland Islands* (1890)

Shipton, Eric *Tierra del Fuego: the Fatal Lodestone* (1973)

South American Missionary Society *Letters of G. Pakenham Despard 1861*

Strange, Ian J. *The Falkland Islands* (1972)

Strange, Ian J. *A Field Guide to the Wildlife of the Falkland Islands* (1992)

Trehearne, Mary Falkland Heritage (1978)

Wolsey, Shane *Old Falklands Photos* (1990)

INDEX

complement,10; Divisions, 14, 21; engine defects, 133; gunnery, 11, 20-21, 23, 127, 151; kelp as navigation aid and hazard, 57, 77, 86; navigation problems, 86, 95, 107, 131, 133; officers, 14, 21, 22 illus; paperwork, 24, 93, 107; provisioning, 15, 85, 95, 98, 107, 111; sailing characteristics, 19, 20-21, 24-26; ship's company, 21, 23 illus, 45, 153; ship's company on horseback, 73; steaming characteristics, 19, 133; storms, 20, 24, 25-26; theatricals, 147; uniform, 17, 22, 150; wardroom activities, 19, 61, 68, 127

Earle, Augustus, 66
East Cove, 57
Edinburgh, Duke of, 74n

Falkland Islanders; British origins, 4; camp houses, 57, 61, 62 illus, 93, 122, 130, 137, 138 illus; character of, 1, 2, 4, 82; at a concert, 50; dress, 59 illus, 60 illus, 72 illus, 73, 132 illus, 138 illus; "home", 53, 62; population, 1, 4; at the races, 71, 73; Scottish influence, 4, 71, 72 illus, 75, 95, 101-102; shearers, 59 illus, 60 illus; shepherds, 72, 95, 138; wages, 2. See also under names of individuals and names of settlements.
Falkland Islands; churches, 5, 71, 149; economic developement, 1, 4; Executive Council, 38; government appointments, 38, 45n; harbour defences, 17, 29; house construction, 52; legal procedures, 38, 56; Legislative Council, 4, 36; meteorology, 52; naval visits, 4, 5; newspapers, 43n, 62; Pax Britannica,

30; philately, 56; schools, 5, 43n; security, 30; terrain, 39, 93, 94, 98. *See also* botany, fishing, horsemanship, ornithology,sealing, ship provisioning, ship repair, wool trade. *See also* under names of settlements.
Falkland Islands Company, 35, 61, 63, 71, 76, 108, 113
Felton, Arthur, 2, 107-108, 109 illus, 110-111
Felton sisters, 89
Fennia, barque, 35 illus
Fennoran (Chief Gunner's Mate), 83, 85
Firefly, HMS, 13, 148
Fishing, 98, 101, 133, 135, 137
Fitzroy, Captain (later Vice Admiral) Robert, 146
Fitzroy Harbour, 148
Foam (nineteenth-century yacht), 112, 113 illus
Foam (present day boat), 97
Fossils, 139
Fox Bay, 133
Fur seals, 98, 99 illus

Gardiner, Commander Allen, 117, 119
Garnet, HMS, 13, 15, 17, 133, 135, 141, 143, 147
George Island, 83
Gilbert, W.S., 20, 142
Goose Green, 71n, 76
Goosing, 131, 135
Government House, 39-42, 40-42 illus
Great Britain, SS, 76
Grenfell, Mr, 15
Guanacos, 57, 58 illus

Halliday family, 138
Hamilton, Dr Samuel, 147
Hamm, Engineer Richard, 21

159

Jane Cameron was born in the Falkland Islands and grew up on the family farm at Port San Carlos. She was educated at boarding school in Sussex and at the University of East Anglia where she took a degree in History and Philosophy. She then trained as a conservator of books, and after a two-year apprenticeship with Sandy Cockerell at the Riversdale Bindery she worked for six years in the Conservation Section of the Bodleian Library in Oxford. She was able to combine her training with her love of Falkland Islands history when in 1989 she took up her present post as Falkland Islands Government Archivist. Introduced to the story of the *Dwarf* by Kit Layman, she immediately shared his enthusiasm, and what began as a search for a few old photographs was soon transformed into an absorbing pursuit of background material to these enchanting letters.

Kit Layman is a retired admiral who has commanded ships of all sizes – from a minehunter the size of H.M.S. *Dwarf*, to the aircraft carrier H.M.S. *Invincible*. His interest in the Falklands originally came from his father, who visited the Islands in World War II and "never stopped talking about it". Layman commanded H.M.S. *Argonaut* and the Seventh Frigate Squadron in the Falklands war of 1982, when his ship was severely damaged by Argentine bombs. Later as a Rear Admiral he served as Commander British Forces Falkland Islands 1986–7. During this period he came across the *Dwarf* story, and subsequently traced letters and photographs – the raw material for this book – to France and the United States. He is now a consultant in telecommunications and maritime affairs, and the author/editor of *Man of Letters*, a biography of Robert Chambers of Edinburgh.

160

NOTICE TO MARINERS.
FALKLAND ISLANDS.—FIXED LIGHT ON CAPE PEMBROKE.

The Colonial Government at the Falkland Islands has given notice that a fixed light of the natural colour was established on Cape Pembroke on the first of December last.

The light stands at a height of 110 feet above the mean level of the sea and is visible in ordinary weather at a distance of 14 miles. It shows a bright fixed light in every direction seaward, but is dark towards Port William, between the bearings of N.W. ½ N. and W.

The Tower is 60 feet high; it is circular, of iron, and painted in white and red bands. It stands in lat. 51° 40′ 43″ S.; lon. 57° 41′ 49″ West of Greenwich. The illuminating apparatus is catoptric or reflecting, and of the first order.

Cape Pembroke, on which a beacon has hitherto stood, forms the easternmost point of the Falkland group, and also the south headland of Port William, within which, on its south side, is Stanley Harbour.

From the Uranie Rock (which lies east one mile from the outer rock off Volunteer Point) the lighthouse bears S. 13° E., or S. by E. ¼ E. nearly, distant 9½ miles. From the centre of the large Wolf Rock, to the southward, the lighthouse bears N. 7° E.

A vessel entering Port William will leave the light on the port hand; and the Master should be careful to observe that, as the flood tide sets strongly to the northward, and the ebb to the southward in passing Cape Pembroke, he should not pass between this Cape and the Seal Rocks (which lie north-east of it about ⅓ mile) unless the ship is under steam or has a good commanding breeze; in light winds or much swell it is better to pass outside.

(All bearings are magnetic. Var. 18¾° E. in 1856.)

By command of their Lordships.
(Signed)   JOHN WASHINGTON,
HYDROGRAPHIC OFFICE, ADMIRALTY, LONDON,   *Hydrographer.*
5th February 1856.

Directions pour naviguer dans le Port de Stanley de

Il y a un Phare d'établi sur le Cap Pembroke, qui forme le poi des Iles Malouines, ainsi que le midi du promontoire de Port Wil trouve du côté du midi le Port Stanley. La Tour, qui est de fe (Anglais); elle est de forme circulaire, vernie de blanc, et se trou 51.40.43 S., Longitude 57.41.49 W. de Greenwich. Le Fanal se dessus de niveau de la mer, et par un temps ordinaire, à la dis Le Phare montre une lumière brillante et non vacillante dans t de la mer, mais il est sombre du côté de Port William entre les ½ N. et W. L'apparat pour l'éclairage est catoptrique ou réverbé

Du Roc Uranie (qui est un mille à l'Est de l'extérieur du Cap V est à la hauteur S. 13° E. ou S. par E. ¼ E. environ, à la distance c centre du grand Roc Wolf, vers le midi, le Phare est à la hauteur

Un Navire entrant dans le Port William doit laisser la lumière o du Port, et le Capitaine doit observer avec soin que comme la mar au Nord, et que le reflux passe par le Cap Pembroke au Sud, il ne d le Cap et les Roca Seal (que se trouvent au Nord-East à environ que le navire ne se trouve sous vapeur, ou qu'il ait une brise favora legers, ou une grosse mer, il vaut mieux passer en dehors.

Stanley est un Port libre. L'eau y est bonne, des provisions f autre espèce et des legumes peuvent s'y procurer. On peut a les navires.

Zur Beachtung für Schiffsführer, welche in Port Stanley auf East Falkland Island einlaufen.

Auf dem Oestlichtsten Punkte der Falkland Inseln, dem Cap Pembroke, und zwar an der Südseite der Einsegelung nach Port William, an dessen südlichen Ufer Port Stanley liegt, ist ein runder eiserner 60 Fuss-hoher Leuchtthurm errichtet, unterm 51.40.43 S. Breite, und 57.41.49 W. Länge von Greenwich, dessen weisses, festes, zurückstrahlendes (katoptrisches) Licht 110 engl: Fuss (bei gewöhnlichem Wasserstande) hoch und bei gutem Wetter 14 Meilen weit sichtbar ist. Es leuchtet seewärts nach allen Richtungen, nur nicht nach Port William zu, zwischen den Höhen von N.W. ½ N. und W.

Nördlich von Port William liegt Volunteer Point und eine Meile östlich von dessen ausserster Klippe Uranie Rock—von Uranie Rock liegt der Leuchtthurm 9½ Meilen S. 13° O. oder S. von O. betnahe ¼ O. Vom Mittelpunkt des grossen Wolf Rock, liegt das Leuchtfeuer N. 7° O. Nach Port William segelnde Schiffe lassen das Feuer Backbord und müssen, wenn sie weder Dampfkraft noch besonders günstigen Wind haben, die Einfahrt zwischen Cap Pembroke und den Seal Rocks vermeiden, weil die Fluth stark nordwärts läuft und die Ebbe südlich Cap Pembroke vorbei strömt. Bei wenig Wind und starken Deining ist es unbedingt richtig die Seal Rocks südlich liegen zu lassen.

Stanley ist ein Freihafen, wo gutes Wasser, frischer Proviant, Gemüse und Waaren aller Art vorräthig sind, auch Schiffe ausgebessert werden.

STANLEY IS A FREE PORT

THE FALKLAND ISLANDS COMPANY'S

Manager at Stanley supplies

Water, Fresh Provisions, Vegetables, Coals, Ship's Stores, and undertakes Shipping Repairs, having a Diving Apparatus, means for Heaving Down and Hulks to receive Cargo.   For Letters of Introduction, Charts, or arrangements for Coaling Steamers, apply at the Company's Offices,

No. 39A, GRACECHURCH STREET, LONDON, E.C.

Cape Pembroke Lighthouse
110 feet high.
Painted in white and red bands.